Abraham

DISCOVER MICHIGAN

By David B. McConnell

Illustrated by
George L. Rasmussen

Hillsdale Educational Publishers, Inc.
Hillsdale, Michigan

ACKNOWLEDGMENTS

I thank the many Michigan teachers and other educators who have assisted me with this project. I especially thank Judy Gillespie, Hillsdale fourth grade teacher, and Dr. Floyd Dain, Central Michigan University professor, for their guidance in developing the text. I am also grateful to Mary Ann Evans and Sue Watson, fourth grade teachers at St. Frances Xavier School, Petoskey; to all the fourth grade teachers at the Comstock elementary schools and the Hanover elementary school; and to Nancy Hanatyk.

Appreciation goes to Karen Hart of the Travel Bureau, Department of Commerce, and to John Curry of the Michigan State Archives for their help in securing photographs for the book. Special thanks go to the staff at Hillsdale Educational Publishers for their patience and many hours of hard work.

A great debt is owed to the artist, George L. Rasmussen. I feel his work is outstanding and gives considerable visual impact to the students.

Most of all, I acknowledge the help and support of my mother and father. Without their patient nurture, I would not have been in a position to write this book. They have provided me with the opportunity to explore my creativity and to educate my mind.

I am deeply interested in the response of teachers and students to this textbook. I shall appreciate receiving any comments concerning the book and its use. These may be sent to my attention, the publisher's address.

David B. McConnell

Published by Hillsdale Educational Publishers,
39 North Street, Box 245, Hillsdale, Michigan 49242.
Printed in the United States of America.

Library of Congress Cataloging in Publication Data

McConnell, David B. (David Barry), 1949-
 Discover Michigan.

 Includes index.
 Summary: An introduction to the state's geography and history, with brief chapters on its agricultural crops, industrial products, and famous people.
 1. Michigan—History—Juvenile literature. 2. Michigan—Biography—Juvenile literature.
[1. Michigan]
I. Rasmussen, George L., ill. II. Title.
F566.3.M33   977.4   81-6722
ISBN 0-910726-07-8   AACR2

third printing

CONTENTS

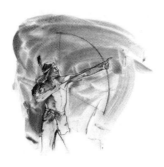

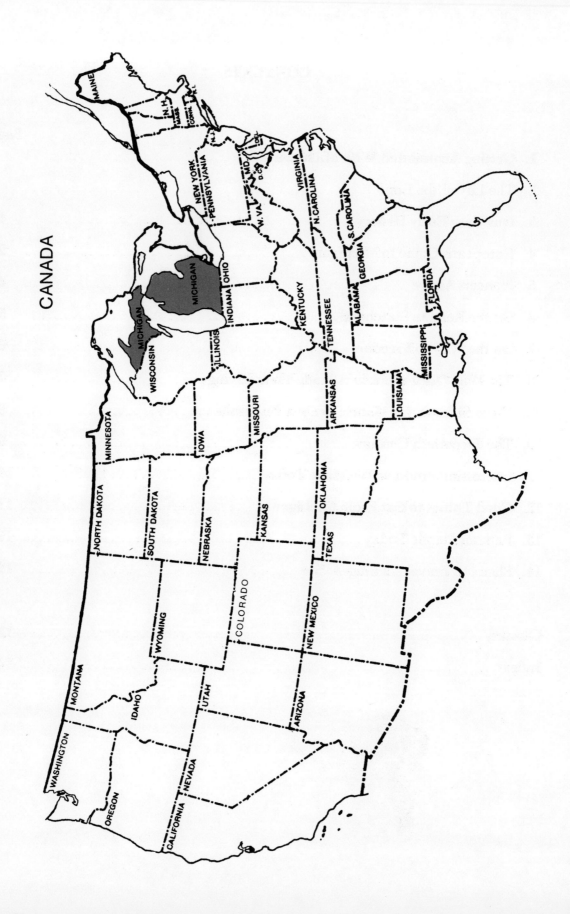

Chapter 1

GETTING ACQUAINTED WITH MICHIGAN

This book will help you discover Michigan, the state where you live. There are certainly many exciting things to discover. Michigan has old forts that were once attacked by the Indians and English soldiers. There are beautiful lakes and giant sand dunes. Huge ships sail around it in the Great Lakes. Open your eyes and start to learn about Michigan! Read about the people and events which make Michigan great. See how the Indians lived long ago. Find out who started the city of Detroit. Learn how iron ore was discovered. Read about the men who made the early cars. Find out how Michigan people helped with the space program.

Have you ever wondered what a state is? What is this very special place we call Michigan?

First of all, a state is an area of land. Each state has its own shape, its own borders and boundaries. Nature and politics helped to make our state's shape. Today we know what land is part of Michigan. This was not always so.

The water of the Great Lakes gives Michigan most of its shape because it is almost all around us. People and politics helped make the shape too. People decided where to draw the boundaries between one state and the next. Sometimes the boundaries follow rivers because it is easy to see where they are, and to know if you have crossed the border. Michigan has three rivers on the border between it and Canada.

Besides being an area of land, a state is the people who live there. All of these people make the history of Michigan. You and I are each a little bit of Michigan. The things we do and what happens to us are all a part of Michigan history. The people who live in Michigan today have their roots in places all over the world. They, or their relatives, have lived in Africa, Asia, Europe, Canada, or Mexico. Some families have been in Michigan even before it was a state. Others have just moved to Michigan. They may have traveled from Mexico, Cuba, Vietnam, Jordan, Lebanon or Syria to make a new home here. They are discovering Michigan for themselves, just as you are.

When large groups of people live together, they always seem to start some kind of government. Michigan has its own state government. Our government is the third part of what a state is.

Michigan is only one of fifty states in the United States. It is in the north central part of the country. It is the only state to border on four of the five Great Lakes. Lake Superior, Lake Michigan, Lake Huron and Lake Erie each touch the land of Michigan. This fact has caused the state often to be called the *Great Lakes State*.

It is also the only state where water divides it into two parts. The northern part is called the *Upper Peninsula*, and the southern part is the *Lower Peninsula*. A peninsula is land surrounded by water on three sides. The water which divides the state into two parts is called the Straits of Mackinac (sounds like MACK-in-aw). It is between the towns of Mackinaw City and St. Ignace (Saint IG-nes). This water is four miles wide, very deep, and it is formed by Lake Michigan and Lake Huron.

Words You Should Know

Here are words you should know before you read chapter 1. There are helps near some of the words so you will know how to say them. The main syllable is printed in capital letters. There may be words you do not understand. If you do not know what a word means, look it up in a dictionary or in the glossary which is in the back of the book. Only the words with the dots are in the glossary.

Africa	Lake Erie	Petoskey (peh-TOS-kee)
Asia	Lake Huron	politics
• Audubon Society	Lake Michigan	relatives
boundaries	Lake Superior	roots
Canada	Latin	• shield
coat of arms	Lebanon	state seal
Cuba	mainland	• Straits of Mackinac (MACK-in-aw)
Europe	Mexico	• symbols
fossil	• Michigama (Mish-ih-GAHM-ah)	Syria
• gem	• motto	waterway
government	peninsula	wolverine
Jordan		

Latin words and phrases: E Pluribus Unum (A PLUR-ih-bus Oo-NUM)
Si Quaeris Peninsulam Amoenam Circumspice (See KWI-rus
PINE-in-sul-am AMOY-nam KER-kum-speh-ka)
Tuebor (TOO-a-bor)

The Lower Peninsula is shaped roughly like a mitten, and in between the thumb and the hand is Saginaw Bay. The Lower Peninsula is about two and one-half times larger than the Upper Peninsula, and it contains twenty times more people.

We have already been reading about Michigan, but do you know what the name means? The word Michigan comes from the Chippewa word, *Michigama*. This word means great lake. Michigan also has nicknames. One name is *Water Wonderland* because we have so many lakes. Then, it is sometimes called the *Wolverine State*. The wolverine is a member of the weasel family, but it is not a small animal. The wolverine is fierce and nasty. Strange as it may seem, probably no wolverines ever lived in Michigan. The nickname *Wolverine State* started a long time ago. It is believed that in the Toledo War, people from Ohio started calling people from Michigan wolverines. They said this because they did not like us. They felt our people were nasty because we wanted the Toledo area.

A Wolverine (Michigan D.N.R.)

Michigan has many things that are unusual and special. Some of these are told about in our state symbols. We have a state bird, a state tree, a state flower, a state fish, a state stone and a state gem. They may be found in other states too, but people here think of them as being special to Michigan.

THE STATE BIRD

The robin is our state bird. It became the state bird in 1931. You may wonder how something becomes a state symbol. Usually the state government votes and says so. In 1931 the Michigan Audubon Society had an election to see which bird our people would choose. The robin won. It was voted to be the best known and best loved of all the birds in Michigan.

THE STATE FLOWER

Our state flower is the apple blossom. It has been the state flower since 1897 when it was voted for by the state government. In the spring the apple blossoms bring beauty to our orchards and farms.

THE STATE TREE

The towering White Pine is our state tree. It is special to Michigan because so many were cut down for lumber long ago. The lumber helped to build houses in our state and many other states. Most of the White Pine trees that are left today are in the Upper Peninsula.

THE STATE FISH

A colorful trout is our state fish. It is the Brook Trout. It is about eight to ten inches long, and it has blue, green and red spots on its sides.

THE STATE STONE

The state stone is the Petoskey Stone. It is called this because many are found on the beaches of Lake Michigan, near the city of Petoskey. This stone is very old and it is really a fossil of coral. You can see a pattern in the stone from the old coral but you may have to look closely.

THE STATE GEM

In 1973 the state government voted to have a state gem. It is the Lake Superior *Greenstone*. It is green, of course. It is most often found on the beaches of Isle Royale. Isle Royale is an island that is part of Michigan and it is far north in the cold waters of Lake Superior.

THE STATE FLAG

Michigan has its own state flag. Have you ever looked closely at one? The first thing you see is that most of the flag is bright blue. In the middle of the flag is the Michigan Coat of Arms. The Coat of Arms is taken from the State Seal. This is not an animal you can see in the zoo. It is a picture which is the official symbol of our

THE STATE TREE (WHITE PINE)

THE STATE BIRD (ROBIN)

THE STATE STONE (PETOSKEY STONE)

THE STATE FLAG

THE STATE FLOWER (APPLE BLOSSOM)

THE STATE FISH (TROUT)

state. The seal was designed by Lewis Cass, a famous Michigan man of long ago. It has an eagle holding arrows and an olive branch in its claws. There is an elk and a moose too. They are next to a shield which has a picture on it. The picture shows a man with one hand raised to mean peace. In his other hand is a gun which means that we will defend our state. There is also a rising sun and a lake in the picture.

The flag has several words on it. You probably will not understand these words because they are Latin. "E Pluribus Unum" means "From many, one." It says this because the United States is formed from many states. Another word on the flag is "Tuebor." It means "I will defend." The third group of words is "Si Quaeris Peninsulam Amoenam Circumspice." This means "If you seek a pleasant peninsula, look about you."

These last words, "If you seek a pleasant peninsula, look about you," are also our state motto.

This is the end of the first chapter. You should have learned many things from this chapter. You should understand what a state is. You should know what the name Michigan means. You should remember what the state symbols are. You should know what is on our state flag, and what our state motto is.

The Michigan State Seal

QUESTIONS TO ANSWER

1. Name the three main things a state is.

2. Give the meaning of the word *Michigan*.

3. What separates the two parts of Michigan?

4. What is the lower part of Michigan shaped like?

5. What is the Michigan state bird?

6. What is the Michigan state flower?

7. What is the Michigan state tree?

8. What is the Michigan state fish?

9. What is the Michigan state stone?

10. What is the Michigan state gem?

11. Tell all the things you can about the Michigan state flag.

12. What does the Michigan state motto mean?

Words You Should Know

Here are words you should know before you read chapter 2.

Baraga (BAR-eh-geh)
- capital
- counties
- courthouse
Drummond Island
- explorer
glaciers
Gogebic Lake (Go-GEE-bik)

Houghton Lake
Kalamazoo (Kal-ah-mah-ZOO)
Lake Charlevoix (SHAR-la-voy)
Manistee (Man-is-TEE)
Manistique Lake (Man-is-TEEK)
Menominee (Meh-NAHM-eh-nee)
Mullet Lake
Muskegon (Mus-KEE-gan)

Saginaw (SAG-i-naw)
St. Joseph (SAYNT JOE-zef)
sand dunes
sawmill
suburbs
Torch Lake
tribe

Chapter 2

THE LAY OF THE LAND

You already know that Michigan has two peninsulas. Do you remember that the Lower Peninsula has a shape like a mitten? It has this shape because of the Great Lakes around it. Keep in mind that Lake Michigan, Lake Huron, Lake Superior and Lake Erie all touch the land of Michigan.

The fifth Great Lake has not been mentioned. It is Lake Ontario, and it does not touch Michigan. If you want to remember the names of all five Great Lakes, you can think of HOMES. Each letter in HOMES is the start of one of the Great Lakes.

Lake Superior is the largest and deepest of the Great Lakes. It is over 1300 feet deep. Its water is very cold all year. There are many shipwrecks that lie on its bottom in the dark, cold water. The water in Lake Superior does not freeze over in the winter, but huge mounds of ice pile up on the shore. Lake Superior is the largest lake of fresh water in the world. Only the oceans and seas filled with salt water are bigger.

See how water is on three sides of the two peninsulas that make Michigan.

8

A Sand Dune (Travel Bureau—Michigan Dept. of Commerce)

Lake Michigan is the only one of the Great Lakes completely inside the United States. The others are all shared with Canada. There are many great sand dunes on our shore of Lake Michigan. Often the wind blows the clean white sand into dunes almost as big as mountains.

Lake Huron was one of the first of the Great Lakes to be discovered by the French explorers. It was named for the Indian tribe living along the shore. It is the second largest Great Lake. Lake Huron also has more islands than any other but most of these are on the Canadian side. Michigan's Mackinac Island and Drummond Island are in Lake Huron.

Lake Erie is one of the smaller Great Lakes. It is between Lake Huron and Lake Ontario. Lake Erie is the shallowest of the Great Lakes, and is farther south than the others.

Can you name the other states that touch Michigan? There are three of them. Ohio and Indiana touch the bottom of the Lower Peninsula. Wisconsin touches the west end of the Upper Peninsula.

Michigan is next to a foreign country. On a map you can see that this is Canada. The people of Michigan have been friendly with the people of Canada for a long time. You can go across the border any time you wish. Many people take vacations in Canada.

Most of the people in Michigan live in cities. Many live in villages or on farms too. The largest city in Michigan is Detroit which is in the Lower Peninsula near Canada. Look on your map and find Detroit. Over a million people live there. It is one of the largest cities in the United States.

9

Michigan

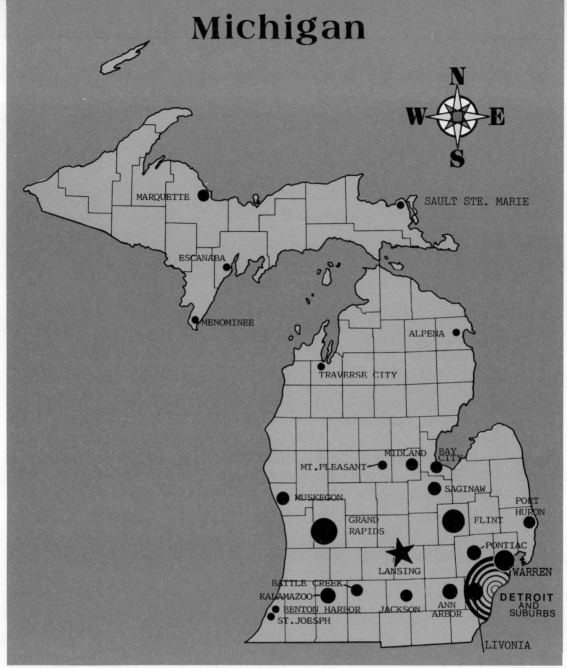

A map with Michigan's larger cities. The bigger the dot, the more people live in that city.

Michigan's second largest city is Grand Rapids. It is in the western part of the Lower Peninsula. Grand Rapids is not nearly as large as Detroit; only about 200,000 people live there.

Warren and Flint are almost the same size. They are our third and fourth largest cities. They have about 160,000 people each. Both of these cities are not far from Detroit. Look on a map and find them. Many of the people in Michigan live in homes in or near Detroit.

The cities in the Upper Peninsula are all smaller than these. In the Upper Peninsula the largest cities are Marquette, Escanaba and Sault Ste. Marie (Soo-Saint-Mar-ee).

Map with the 83 counties in Michigan.

Michigan is divided into many counties. You can see these counties on a state map. Most of them look like little boxes on the map and there are 83 all together. Each has its own name. Keweenaw County is the farthest north. Wayne County is where Detroit is; it has the most people. Other counties are named after different things. Iron County has iron mines. Chippewa County is named after an Indian tribe. Jackson is named after a president of the United States.

Find the county you live in. Do you know its name? You should learn it. Check to see what counties touch the one you live in.

A county is like a little state in many ways. Each one has its own capital, called the county seat. A courthouse is at the county seat. Court is held there and many records are kept in the courthouse.

How a cut through the earth of Michigan might look.

THE LAND UNDER OUR FEET

Many people never think about the ground they walk on or what is under it. The minerals under the ground are very important to Michigan. Several things are mined in Michigan. We get copper, iron and salt from under the ground. Oil and natural gas are found here too, and these help heat our homes and factories. The oil is also made into gasoline for our cars. Limestone comes from under the ground and is used as a building material.

The ground and soil are valuable by themselves. The right kind of soil helps certain crops grow. Farming is a major business in our state. Many types of foods are grown and animals raised.

12

THE GLACIERS—NATURE'S BULLDOZERS OF ICE

Thousands of years ago bulldozers of ice scraped over Michigan. The ice was hundreds and maybe thousands of feet thick. It crushed everything in its way. Plants and trees were crushed. Hills were wiped away and lakes were filled in. The land was covered with ice for a long time. The ice came slowly from the north in Canada until it covered Michigan. It started because the summers were not long enough to melt all of the snow. Each year the mountain of snow became larger and heavier. The great weight of the ice and snow pushed the edges south. Finally, Michigan was covered, also some of Ohio and Indiana.

Very, very slowly it started to melt. A great deal of water was left by the glacier. This water filled in the low places. Many lakes were left behind. Scientists believe the Great Lakes were started by the last glacier as it changed the land and left its water. Over a long time several glaciers moved over Michigan.

The glaciers did other things to Michigan too. In some places they scratched big rocks. Once in a while you can see the marks left by the ice thousands of years ago. The last glacier left much dirt behind. Most of it ended up in the southern part of the Lower Peninsula. This dirt helped to make the crops grow better there. Often the piles of dirt were as big as hills. This is one reason the Lower Peninsula is so hilly in places. The glacier helped to make Michigan the way it is today.

Michigan has hills and valleys. It is not flat as it looks to be on the maps. It has ups and downs. The highest place is Mt. Curwood. It is 1,980 feet high. Mt. Curwood is in Baraga County. Be a detective and try to find Baraga County on a map. The lowest part of our state is the shore of Lake Erie.

Some of the hilliest land is near the shore of Lake Superior in the western Upper Peninsula. Some of the flattest land is near Saginaw in the Saginaw Valley of the Lower Peninsula.

THE RIVERS AND INLAND LAKES

We have many other lakes and rivers. Rivers are nice to use for boating and canoeing. But they are important for other reasons too. They drain the water from the land, and carry it to the Great Lakes. This keeps the land from becoming a swamp.

The rivers were important to the Indians too. They paddled their canoes up and down them. This was easier than walking through the thick woods. The first explorers used them too. Many years ago lumbermen cut down the trees and floated them on the rivers. The rivers carried the logs to the sawmills.

Michigan's largest rivers are the Grand, Kalamazoo, Manistee, Menominee, Muskegon, Saginaw and St. Joseph. The Menominee River is in the Upper Peninsula. Try to find these rivers on the map on the next page.

PORTAGE LAKE

LAKE GOGEBIC

MANISTIQUE LAKE

MENOMINEE RIVER

BURT LAKE MULLET LAKE

LAKE CHARLEVOIX
TORCH LAKE

HOUGHTON
LAKE

MANISTEE RIVER

MUSKEGON RIVER

GRAND RIVER

SAGINAW RIVER

KALAMAZOO
RIVER

ST. JOSEPH
RIVER

The larger inland lakes and rivers in Michigan. The Grand River is the longest.
The Saginaw River is short but it carries a great deal of water.

There are many inland lakes in Michigan—about 11,000 in all. They are called inland lakes because they are inside the land area of the state. They are not part of the Great Lakes. Some of the big inland lakes are on the map. Houghton Lake is the largest of all. Find it on the map.

These lakes are wonderful for fishing and boating. There are many nice cottages on the shores of these and other lakes in our state.

Chapter Review:

In this chapter you should have learned these important things:
a. the shape of the state
b. the names of the five Great Lakes
c. the name of the foreign country next to Michigan
d. the names of Michigan's two largest cities
e. the name of the county where you live

QUESTIONS TO ANSWER

1. What is the meaning of peninsula?

2. Name the five *Great Lakes.*

3. Three states touch Michigan. Give the names of these states.

4. Most of us live in cities. Name the two largest cities in Michigan.

5. How many counties are in Michigan?

6. In which county do you live?

7. Which counties touch yours?

8. Limestone and salt are two minerals that come from where?

9. Of what were the glaciers made?

10. What did the glaciers do to Michigan land?

11. What helped form the *Great Lakes* as they are today?

12. What is the highest place in Michigan?

13. How many inland lakes are there in Michigan?

14. Name four of the largest rivers in Michigan.

Words You Should Know

Here are words you should know before you read chapter 3.

- Algonquian (Al-GON-kwee-in)
  axes
- birch bark
  canoe
- ceremonies
  Chippewa (CHIP-eh-wah)
- elk
  Europeans
  gill nets
  Hiawatha
  Huron

Iroquois (EAR-a-kwoi)
Manitou (MAN-i-too)
mastodons (MASS-ta-dons)
Miami (My-AM-ee)
missionaries
museums
Native Americans
Ojibwa (O-JIB-wa)
Ottawa (OT-ah-wah)
Potawatomi (POT-a-WAT-o-me)
- pouches
- rawhide

religion
sap
Sauk (sounds like talk—but
  uses *s* in place of the *t*)
spiritual
- stockade
- sturgeon (STIR-jen)
- tipis (TEE-pees)
  valuable
- warriors
  wigwam
  Wyandotte (WY-n-dot)

This is one of the new freighters on the Great Lakes. It is 1,000 feet long and over 100 feet wide.
(Pickands Mather and Company)

16

Chapter 3

OUR VERY EARLY HISTORY

Have you ever found a fossil in a rock? A fossil is any trace, print or remains of a plant or animal from very, very long ago. A fossil could be a piece of bone from an animal. It could be a shell or the print of a leaf in stone. All of these would be many thousands or millions of years old. Often the remains have been changed to stone by minerals in the ground.

Fossils are clues about the far past. Michigan's state stone is a fossil. It is the Petoskey Stone. Do you remember that it is a fossil of coral? This tells us that long ago Michigan was covered by a sea.

Fossils can tell us much about the way Michigan once was. They can tell about what animals lived here, even before man lived here. Some very unusual fossils have been found in Michigan. People discovered fossils of an animal that looked like an elephant. Long curved tusks have been uncovered. Scientists believe these animals were quite hairy. They have called them mastodons. Many, many years ago they lived over most of Michigan. There are none left today. They have all died. We do not know why they died, but today they are gone.

Sometimes other clues about the past are found. A farmer may be plowing a field and uncover an arrowhead. It might be a thousand years old. An Indian might have shot it at a deer or a bear. Over the years the wooden arrow rotted away and left the arrowhead behind.

THE FIRST PEOPLE IN MICHIGAN

Who were the first people in Michigan? Today we call them Indians. We could also call them Native Americans because they were the first people here. They formed groups called tribes. Several different tribes lived in Michigan.

Scientists believe the first people started to live here about 13,000 years ago. People could not have lived in Michigan much before then. Why? The land was covered by the glacier of ice. About this time we think the glacier started to melt. Then the Native American Indians moved into Michigan. That is why we say the first people started to live here about 13,000 years ago.

A mastodon being hunted by an early Indian.

18

They did not use the name, *Indians*, for themselves. They used names like Ottawa (OT-ah-wah) or Chippewa (CHIP-eh-wah) for their tribes. The first Europeans who came here called them *Indians*. The Europeans used this name because they were lost! They thought they had found India. After sailing west a long time they were sure this was India, not America. The Indians should have been called *Americans*.

Two of the tribes in Michigan have been mentioned. The others are the Huron, Potawatomi (POT-a-WAT-o-me) and Miami (My-AM-ee). The Chippewa tribe was known by two names. The other name was Ojibwa (O-JIB-wa). The Huron also had another name which was Wyandotte (WY-n-dot). There were five main tribes altogether. These were the tribes living here about the time the Europeans came.

Another large tribe lived here before them, called the Sauk (sounds like talk, but use an *s* in place of the *t*). This tribe lived in the middle of the Lower Peninsula, near Saginaw. Saginaw means "the place of the Sauk." In the 1600's the Sauk were forced out by other tribes. Once they were attacked by at least two thousand warriors in a terrible battle. We really don't know the reason why all of this happened.

Often the tribes moved their homes. The places where the tribes lived about 1760 are on a map for you.

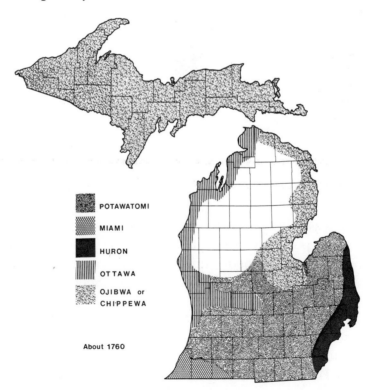

POTAWATOMI

MIAMI

HURON

OTTAWA

OJIBWA or CHIPPEWA

About 1760

This map shows where the Indian tribes lived in Michigan. The tribes did move from time to time.

The three tribes, Potawatomi, Ottawa and Chippewa all spoke the same language. This language was known as Algonquian (Al-GON-kwee-in). The Huron tribe spoke a different language. It was that of the Iroquois (EAR-a-kwoi) tribes. The Miami tribe's language was close to the Algonquian.

HIAWATHA—A Legend From The Past

Hiawatha was not a real person. This is the name given to an Indian in legends. Hiawatha was a very strong, brave and wise Indian leader. His name was made famous in a poem by the poet, Longfellow. The poem is called *Song of Hiawatha*. The idea for the poem came to Longfellow after he had read some Indian legends that were written down by Henry Schoolcraft who lived in Michigan.

If you read the poem about Hiawatha, you will find several places in Michigan mentioned. These places are Lake Superior, the Tahquamenon River and Sugar Loaf Mountain on Mackinac Island.

Today, there is a Hiawatha National Forest in the Upper Peninsula.

An Indian looking at an animal trap he has built.

Chief Keokuk of the Sauk Tribe.

The Potawatomi, Ottawa and Chippewa tribes were alike in many ways. Sometimes they are grouped together and called the Three Fires.

Long ago when the tribes lived here alone, before the Europeans came, there were not many people in Michigan. Maybe there were 100,000 or so people in the Michigan tribes and those nearby. One reason there were so few people is that it took much land to supply food. Most of the food came from hunting and fishing. It took many animals and fish to feed a family. If there were too many Native Americans living near each other, the animals for food would soon be gone. The early tribes did not live in large villages. The need for many animals for food is one reason why.

The tribes used spears and arrows to kill the animals they hunted. Bear, elk, deer, beaver, rabbits and squirrels were some of the animals used for food. Many, many years ago the early Indians hunted the mastodon. They also used traps to catch the smaller animals. Their traps were made of natural things. They might set a big log on a little stick so that it was just about ready to fall. Then some bait would be put near the stick. An animal trying to get the bait would move the stick and then be crushed by the falling log. Sometimes traps would work but many times traps would not catch the animals. There would then be no food that day.

Some of the tribes planted crops and had small farms. This allowed them to have different things to eat with their meat. Planting crops was more important for another reason. The tribes could be more sure of a supply of food if they grew it. They could also store some of the crops for the winter. When crops were planted, more people could live closer together. The tribes did not have to move so often to follow the animals they hunted.

BEAR   WOLF   DEER

Indians were experts at following animal tracks.

Corn, beans, squash and sunflowers were four of the main crops of Michigan's tribes. Sometimes tobacco was grown for smoking. Corn was very important. It was cooked in many ways and it could be made into bread too.

Some tribes farmed more than others, but hunting was still important. Hunting gave the tribes furs and skins for their clothes. The furs were valuable because of Michigan's cold winters.

Fish was a major food of most tribes. The Indians used spears for large fish, such as the sturgeon. A sturgeon may weigh sixty pounds. Hooks and lines and nets were also used. Fishing through the ice was done in the winter. The fish, like other meat, could be dried to keep it from spoiling. Remember, the tribes had no refrigerators or any of the modern appliances we take for granted.

The Chippewa living near Lake Superior gathered wild rice. The rice grew in shallow lakes. It was an important crop for this tribe. All of the tribes ate berries and other wild plants.

Collecting maple sap to make maple syrup was important to the Indians too. Maple trees can live to be two hundred years old. It is possible that maple syrup you eat today could come from the same tree that was used by an Indian long ago.

An Indian fishing from his canoe.

Indian village and wigwam.

HOMES AND SHELTERS

You know that the tribes did not live in houses as we do today. A large house would not have been useful for most tribes. They needed to move often to find better hunting, fishing or firewood.

Tribes in the western states lived in tipis (TEE-pees). These were made of animal skins over long poles. The poles were tied at the top. Most Michigan tribes did not live in tipis. Sometimes they put the poles together like a tipi, but they used tree bark to cover the outside. Michigan tribes often used a wigwam made of birch bark. The birch bark was fastened to bent poles. The wigwam looked like an upside down bowl with a door. The birch bark could be taken off and carried to make a new home. Sometimes other tree bark was used for covering.

The Huron tribe did build larger homes. This tribe often stayed in one place much longer. These homes might have been big enough for twenty families. The largest may have been 150 feet long and 36 feet wide. They were made with wooden poles and covered with bark. Inside would be many fires for cooking and heat. The smoke went through holes in the roof. There could have been walls inside to separate families.

Because of their large homes, the Huron could not move as easily as other tribes. They had larger settlements. Sometimes they put a stockade of wooden posts around several houses which were almost like a fort. The stockade was for protection because sometimes other tribes did attack. Most of the food for the Huron came from farming, so it was not so important to move their homes.

ALL MUST WORK

The women worked at home while the men hunted. The women would clean and get the animals that had been killed ready to eat. They would take care of the crops. They also had to watch the children and make clothes from the furs and animal skins. Tribal women had few tools to use for their work. They did not even have metal pots or pans. Instead there were wooden bowls and spoons. There would have been clay pots to cook food in, if they did not break. Corn was ground in large hollow logs or with stones. If there was sewing to do, the only thing that could be used would be a bone needle and strips of animal hide.

Buckets of birch bark were used for gathering berries. Small pouches made of animal skins were used to hold little things. These women had to be smart and use all the things they could find.

The hunter was very necessary too. If the men did not hunt or fish most of the time, the family would starve. Often the hunter would have to walk or go by canoe long distances to find food. It was a lot of work and took great skill. It also could be very dangerous. A bear might kill a hunter, or a deer could charge and cause a bad wound.

RELIGION

When the French explorers came to Michigan, they brought missionaries with them. The missionaries wanted to bring religion to the tribes. The French felt the tribes did not have any religion. The truth was that they did not have the French religion, but one of their own.

The tribes were quite spiritual. Each tribe had its own beliefs. The Indians did not go to church each Sunday. Often they did talk to their God. They felt the Great Spirit spoke to them in dreams. They believed everything had a spirit, even the rocks, trees and animals. The word, *Manitou*, (MAN-i-tou as in too) was their name for the spirit in things. The *Great Manitou* was a name for their God, the one who made all things. Indian legend says that Mackinac Island was the home of the Great Manitou. They also called the Great Manitou, *Gitchi Manitou*. The legend says the Great Spirit lived alone on the island. Dead chiefs and their families were brought there to be buried and protected by Gitchi Manitou. The Indians came to the island filled with wonder and often left gifts for the God.

It was thought each person had a soul. When the person died, the soul followed a trail over the Milky Way in the sky. Somewhere among the stars was their heaven.

The tribes had special ceremonies for the dead. The dead were often buried with things to help them in the spirit world. A man might be buried with his bow and arrows. A woman might be buried with a wooden bowl or something pretty that was special to her.

Now you know something about the tribes who lived in our state. There is much more you could learn, and you can read about them in other books.

Starting in the middle of the 1600's great changes came to the tribes. This happened because the Europeans came here. The tribes would never be the same again.

Chapter Review:

In this chapter you should have learned these important things:
    a. what a mastodon was
    b. which early Indian tribes lived here
    c. what some of the Indian foods were
    d. what a wigwam is
    e. what name was used by the tribes for their God

QUESTIONS TO ANSWER

1. Sometimes a stone may have the print of an animal track or a leaf in it. What are these special stones called?

2. What animal from Michigan's past looked almost like an elephant?

3. How long have people been living in Michigan?

4. How did the first people here get the name *Indians?*

5. What Native American tribes have lived in Michigan?

6. Where in Michigan did each tribe live?

7. What language did each tribe speak?

8. What food did the tribes have to eat and how did they get it?

9. Describe the homes and shelters used by the tribes.

10. Who was the Great Manitou? Tell why the Great Manitou was important.

Words You Should Know

Here are words you should know before you read chapter 4.

Americans
• archaeology (ARK-ee-oll-o-jee)
brandy
Brule, Etienne (Broo-LAY, Ay-TYEN)
buckskin
Cadillac (Cad-i-lak)
Christians
• customs
Griffin (sometimes Griffon)
Illinois
• Jesuit (JES-oo-it)
Jolliet, Louis (Zhol-ee-ay)
Kentucky
lacrosse

L'Anse (LANS)
LaSalle (La-SAL)
Louisiana
Marquette, Jacques
   (Mar-KETT, Jhahk or Peer)
Menard, Father (MAY-nar)
Michilimackinac
   (MISH-ill-ih-mack-in-aw)
Mississippi
Missouri
Montreal (MONT-ray-al)
Nicolet, Jean (Nee-ko-LAY, Jhan)
North America
ordained

• partridge
Pontiac (PON-tee-ak)
priest
Quebec (Kay-bec)
reunion
• revolution
St. Ignace
   (Saynt IG-nes)
St. Lawrence
Sault Ste. Marie
   (Soo Saynt Ma-REE)
scalps
snowshoes

French explorers travel to Michigan.

Chapter 4

EUROPEANS COME TO MICHIGAN

Europe is made up of several countries. France, Spain, Germany and Holland are in Europe. England is in Europe too. Sometimes England is called Britain or Great Britain.

The first Europeans to visit Michigan were from France. Etienne Brule (Ay-TYEN Broo-LAY) is thought to have been the first French explorer to reach this area. It was in about 1620 when he visited the shores of Lake Superior next to the Upper Peninsula.

The French sailed across the Atlantic Ocean, a long and hard trip. Then they would sail up the St. Lawrence River. Find the St. Lawrence River on a map. The explorers could go as far as Lake Ontario. They had to stop when they reached the Niagara Falls. These falls are at the far end of Lake Ontario. The falls are there because Lake Erie is much higher than Lake Ontario. This made it harder to reach Michigan.

The French set up their first forts on the St. Lawrence River. They had forts at Quebec and Montreal. Today these are large cities in Canada. It was from these forts that the French went west to Michigan. They could not go into Lake Erie unless they unloaded their boats and carried everything around Niagara Falls. The French did find smaller rivers that would let them go into Lake Huron. The Ottawa River was one of these.

When the French followed this river, they came to the northern part of Lake Huron. This was far to the north of Lake Erie. Since the French traveled this way, their first settlements here were in northern Michigan. These settlements were at Sault Ste. Marie (Soo SAYNT-ma-REE) and St. Ignace. These towns are in our Upper Peninsula. They were started in 1668 and 1671. (See map on page 36)

WHY DID THEY COME HERE?

You may have asked yourself why did the French come all the way to Michigan? They came for three reasons. The first one was they came to look for a shortcut to India and China. They wanted to go there so they could buy spices, silk and tea.

They did not have these things in Europe. The French first thought they could reach India and China through the Great Lakes. They thought the world was much smaller than it is.

They also came to make money. They could take furs from the animals and sell them in Europe. The Europeans liked to use the furs in their clothes and hats. Beaver fur was the most wanted.

They came to spread word of their religion too. Several missionaries came to tell the tribes about God. The French felt strongly that they should do this.

The French, then, came for three reasons: First—to find a way to China and India; second—to trade for furs to sell; third—to spread word about their religion.

LIFE CHANGES FOR THE TRIBES

When the French first arrived, most of the tribes were friendly. The French had made some enemies with the Iroquois though. This tribe lived east of Michigan in Canada. The fighting with the Iroquois is another reason they did not want to go through Lake Erie. The Iroquois tribe lived along this lake.

The French traded things to the tribes for furs. They traded beads and blankets. They traded metal pots and steel knives. They also traded guns and gunpowder. The tribes used the beads to make their buckskin clothes beautiful. They liked the blankets to keep them warm in the winter. The metal pots and knives made work much easier for the women of the tribes. The guns made hunting much easier for the men.

The Indians and the French thought trading was good because they each got something they wanted. Soon the Indians found it was hard to get along without their new things. It was very hard to make a trap for a bear, or to spear one for food or fur. It was much better to shoot one with a French rifle. The gunpowder was used up quickly and was always needed. So, more animals were trapped for their fur which could be traded. Before the French arrived, the tribes only killed as many animals as they needed. Now they killed many more for trading. There were fewer beaver and other animals each year.

The way the Indians had lived for so long began to change. More time was spent trapping and trading. The tribes moved closer to the French settlements. This way they could trade more easily. Less time was spent farming as the Indians could even trade for food from the French. The tribes lived more and more in each

30

The Fur Trading Post.

other's land. The customs they once had followed became mixed with customs from other tribes. Their lives were not stable anymore. The young Indians did not honor the old ways.

Finally, when the animals were practically gone, the tribes did not know what to do. They could not trade for the things they needed anymore. The Native Americans became very poor and hungry. This was not their fault. The Indians were smart people, but they were not prepared for the changes caused by the Europeans. They depended on things which they could not control or make for themselves.

As more pioneers moved into Michigan, they wanted the Indians' land. Slowly, pieces of land were given up through treaties with the settlers. It was not too long before the tribes did not have claim to any land here.

Often this did not satisfy the settlers. They did not even want the Indians to live in Michigan. Large numbers of Indians were forced to move out west.

Some did stay though. The United States government set up special areas where they could live. These are known as reservations. There are several in Michigan. There is one near Mt. Pleasant, and others are in the northern part of the state.

Most Indians today do not live on reservations. They live and work in cities and on farms. The tribes do try to keep their customs and old ways alive for their children and grandchildren to remember.

In the last few years the tribes have tried to get back the rights given to them in the old treaties. At least one treaty stated they could fish all they wanted. But some people think this would be bad and too many fish would be taken. So, the tribes are still struggling for their way of life and their rights as the first Michiganians.

WHAT DID THE TRIBES LEAVE US?

The tribes of Michigan had helped the French many times. They had taught these early explorers and fur traders how to live in our cold winters. The French learned how to canoe up and down our rivers. They learned how to make snowshoes from the Native Americans.

The Indians also left us many things we use even today. Foods, such as corn and squash, were first grown by the tribes. The canoe, the snowshoe and the toboggan were all Indian inventions.

The Indians left us the name of our state, *Michigan.* It comes from an Indian word. There are many places in Michigan that have Indian names. The city of Pontiac is named for a chief. Saginaw is named after the Sauk tribe. Kalamazoo is

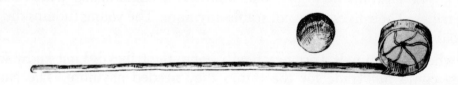

This is a lacrosse racket and ball. Lacrosse is an Indian game still played today.

Snowshoes are one invention left by the Indians.

from a tribal word. Alpena is an Indian word for partridge. Menominee is the name of a tribe from the Upper Peninsula. Our state would not be what it is today without the Native Americans and their tribes.

BRAVE FRENCHMEN WHO CAME TO MICHIGAN

As time passed, more French moved into our state. In 1634 Jean Nicolet (JHAN Nee-ko-LAY) canoed to the land near Green Bay. On his way he went through the Straits of Mackinac. He was probably the first European to do this. It is reported that he came ashore near the bay wearing a Chinese robe. He fired his pistols in the air. This made a real show for the Indians. Some say he thought he had found Asia. This may not be true. It is hard to say. But it did impress the tribes.

Father Menard (MAY-nar), one of the missionaries, preached to the Ottawa near Keweenaw Bay. Father Jacques Marquette (JHAHK Mar-KETT) was working with the Ottawa tribe too. Later he went with the explorer, Jolliet (Zhol-ee-AY) to find the Mississippi River.

FATHER JACQUES (PERE) MARQUETTE—
A Brave Priest in a New Land (born 1637—died 1675)

Jacques Marquette (sometimes known as Pere Marquette) was born in 1637 to a highly respected family in northern France. When he was seventeen he decided to become a Jesuit (JEZ-oo-it) priest. He studied long and hard for this. In 1666 he was ordained and became a priest.

His greatest wish was to become a missionary in America. He wanted to bring his religion to the tribes. He felt this would be a great adventure. At last he was sent to Quebec, in Canada. Father Marquette sailed across the Atlantic and up the St. Lawrence River. Later he traveled to our Upper Peninsula.

He studied the Indian languages and worked hard to convert the tribes. Many among the Ottawa and Huron tribes became Christians because of his work.

Marquette started two missions with little churches. These were at Sault Ste. Marie and St. Ignace.

Marquette knew a young fur trader named Louis Jolliet. In 1672, he asked Marquette to come with him. He was going to explore a great river that went to the south. This was the Mississippi River. Marquette could speak to the tribes on the way.

In May, 1673, they started on their trip. They had two birch bark canoes and their supplies. They paddled around Lake Michigan to Green Bay, Wisconsin. They went up several rivers to the west. Often they had to carry their canoes around waterfalls and rapids. Finally, they reached the Mississippi. They were the first Europeans to see this part of the river. The two men followed the river for over six hundred miles, but they did not reach the mouth. They turned back to come home. The trip had been very hard and Marquette became ill. He left Michigan the next winter to visit Indians in Illinois. His illness grew worse. He was so sick he knew he was going to die. He started back to the mission at St. Ignace. Marquette did not make it back, and he died near the shore of Lake Michigan. He was buried near a river; this river was named after him. It is called the Pere Marquette. Two years later, some of his Indian friends took his body back to the mission at St. Ignace.

A man named LaSalle built the first sailboat on the upper Great Lakes. It was named the *Griffin*. (Sometimes you will see this name spelled *Griffon*.) On its first trip in the Great Lakes it disappeared and was not heard from again. You will read more about the Griffin later.

These were some of the first Europeans in our state. They came here with their own dreams for the land they found. They claimed the land for France. Some of these people tried to find a way to Asia. Others looked for gold but found valuable furs instead. Some came to tell the tribes about God. A few of these brave men died here, while others went on to explore more of America. They were all an important part of our past.

FIRST TOWNS IN OUR STATE

The missionaries started missions and churches. Two of these were at Sault Ste. Marie and St. Ignace. A third was at L'Anse (Lans) in the western Upper Peninsula. These were all started in the late 1600's.

New forts were built. The first fort was Fort Miami which is where the city of St. Joseph is today. Another early fort was built near Port Huron. In 1701 a fort was built at Detroit. This was the beginning of our largest city today. It was started by Cadillac (CAD-i-lak). In 1715 Fort Michilimackinac (MISH-ill-ih-mack-in-naw) was built at the tip of the Lower Peninsula. By 1751 the French had built seven forts in Michigan.

HOW WE KNOW ABOUT THE PAST

How do we know what the French were doing so long ago? First of all, there were reports sent back to France. Some of these were saved. Stories were told from one person to another. The missionaries wrote down things that happened to them. Some of their records were saved. We also know because scientists have been digging at Fort Michilimackinac. They have found many small things that give us clues about the people there. They have found parts of the old fort buildings.

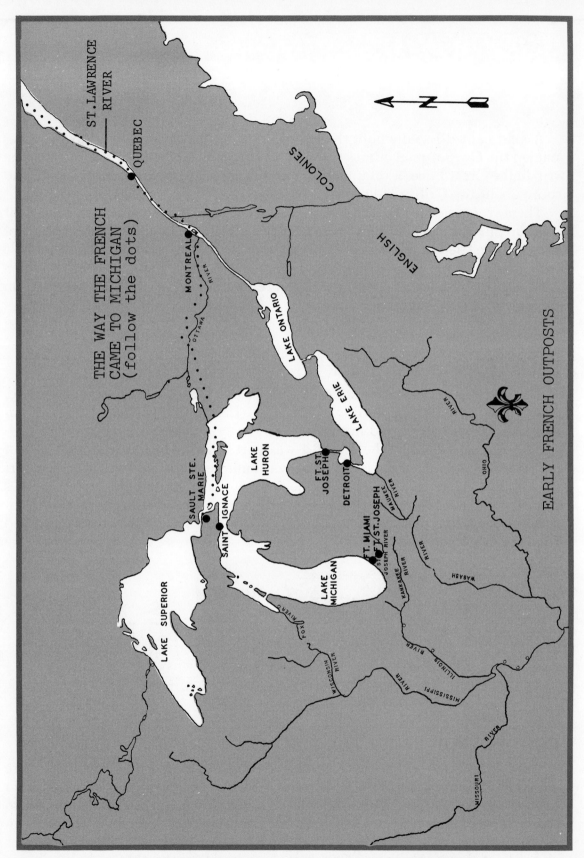

THE WAY THE FRENCH CAME TO MICHIGAN (follow the dots)

ST. LAWRENCE RIVER

QUEBEC

MONTREAL

OTTAWA RIVER

ENGLISH COLONIES

LAKE ONTARIO

LAKE ERIE

SAULT STE. MARIE

SAINT IGNACE

LAKE HURON

FT. ST. JOSEPH

DETROIT

MAUMEE RIVER

ST. JOSEPH

FT. MIAMI

ST. JOSEPH RIVER

KANKAKEE RIVER

RIVER

OHIO

WABASH

LAKE SUPERIOR

LAKE MICHIGAN

FOX RIVER

WISCONSIN RIVER

ILLINOIS RIVER

MISSISSIPPI RIVER

MISSOURI RIVER

EARLY FRENCH OUTPOSTS

This map shows the way some of the French came to Michigan.

CADILLAC—The Man Who Started Detroit (born about 1656—died 1730)

Cadillac was born in France. His father was a judge and owned some land. His life was not an easy one though. His father spent most of his money to get another son out of trouble.

Cadillac had to join the French army in order to get an education. He was not very good looking and he had a long nose. He was also known to have a hot temper. But he was able to impress the king. He was good with a sword; he was honest and courageous.

In 1683 the king sent Cadillac to America. After a while, he came to Michigan, and he was put in charge of the post at Mackinac. Later, he started the fort that grew to be Detroit. Cadillac brought his wife and two sons to Detroit. His wife and another woman traveled by canoe from Quebec. They were some of the first European women to come to Michigan. His wife was a brave person to make such a difficult trip.

Some of the French leaders here were jealous of Cadillac. They asked the king to send him away. Foolishly, the king listened. He sent Cadillac to Louisiana. This was in 1713. After four difficult years there, he retired and went back to France.

They have found buttons, clay pipes used for smoking, bullets and other objects. This work of digging for clues from the past is called archaeology (ARK-ee-oll-o-jee). It is important to our understanding of the past.

The French forts were built for a reason. They wanted to protect their land. The fur trade was important to them. The forts protected them from the tribes just in case a fight started. But the French were worried more about another enemy. This enemy had many guns and cannon too! They were worried about the English!

FRENCH AND INDIAN WAR

The French and the English had been fighting in Europe for some time. About 1755 the English decided to push the French out of North America. The English had colonies on the east coast. Soldiers were sent west to attack the French.

The French were not weak, but they were surprised at Quebec. Quebec is on the St. Lawrence River, and it was an important fort for the French. If it were lost to the English, they could not send supplies down the river. Without supplies they would have to leave the places in the West, such as Michigan. The battle at Quebec was a large one, but the French lost. Later they lost Montreal.

THE ENGLISH ARRIVE

In 1760 English soldiers marched into the fort at Detroit. The French gave up without a shot. This war was between the French and English, but was called the French and Indian War. Actually, the French and Indians were fighting together against the English. If the French had won this war, life might be much different in Michigan today. We could all be speaking French! Canada would belong to France too! Because the French were the first to come to this part of America, some people in Canada do speak French. They also have French customs.

When the French left Michigan, many of the Indians were upset. They did not have anyone with whom they could trade furs. They wanted the rifles, the gunpowder, the blankets and other trade goods. The English did not see the tribes as friends because they had been fighting them and the French. After a while, they traded a little with the tribes. The tribes did not get very much for their furs though, so they decided to fight.

This war could have made a big difference for Michigan too. This was Chief Pontiac's War on the English. If the tribes had beaten the English, it could have long delayed settlers from coming to this area. Perhaps they would never have come at all.

CHIEF PONTIAC ATTACKS

Some Indian leaders said the English should be driven out of the country. Chief Pontiac of the Ottawa Tribe planned an attack on the English forts. The year was 1763. Several tribes were to attack at the same time. They attacked the fort at Michilimackinac. They had a very good plan. The Indians would come to the fort to play a game of lacrosse. Lacrosse is played with a small ball and long handled rackets. There are two teams with several players. The ball is tossed or carried with a racket. The Indians enjoyed playing lacrosse, and the English

Indians attack the English at Fort Michilimackinac.

soldiers liked to watch. They would seem to be very friendly. An Indian would toss the ball into the open gate of the fort, and more Indians would run in to get it. Then the attack would start. The women would have guns under their blankets. The warriors would grab the guns and start shooting the English soldiers. This plan worked, and the fort was taken.

Pontiac's plan for the fort at Detroit was different. He and several others asked to come into the fort. He said he wanted to talk of peace. Pontiac and his men had cut the barrels of their rifles short. The short guns were under their blankets. Once inside they planned to attack; but when Pontiac and his men got inside the fort, they were surprised to find the English ready. Each soldier had several pistols or rifles ready to shoot.

It seems a French trader's daughter had heard of the plan to attack the fort. The French wanted the tribes to win, but this girl was in love with one of the English men. She did not know what to do. Finally, she told the English about the plan, and she saved her boyfriend.

During the meeting Pontiac talked briefly and then asked to leave. The English let the Indians go; probably because they did not have room for so many prisoners. They also hoped Pontiac would be scared and would give up any other plans.

Later, Pontiac did attack the fort from the outside. The fight lasted many months, but Pontiac could not win. Ships were able to bring supplies to the back of the fort for the English. After a long time, Pontiac left. The tribes had fought well. Many other forts were taken, but in the end, the English stayed.

THE CHIEF'S FRIEND

After some time had passed, Chief Pontiac moved west. Before he did this, he made friends with an unusual man named Jean de Sable (Jhan Day-SAW-bul).

Jean de Sable was a Black man who was born in Haiti. Haiti is an island not too far from Cuba. Jean de Sable went to school in France, and later moved to New Orleans. About this time the Spanish took over New Orleans; so, he traveled north and finally arrived in Michigan.

De Sable made his home near Chief Pontiac's camp. It is said they became close friends. De Sable traded furs with the Indians. He also explored parts of Michigan. The little town of Au Sable and the Au Sable River are named after him. These are in the northeastern part of the Lower Peninsula.

When Pontiac did go west, de Sable followed. Later, he started a trading post where Chicago is today. Jean de Sable, the Black Frenchman, was probably the first settler in Chicago. He married while he lived in the Chicago area. His wife was a beautiful Potawatomi girl.

This Black man was one of the first in the Michigan territory. He led an exciting life and made friends with the Indians, English and later the Americans.

PONTIAC—Indian Chief and Leader of the Tribes (born about 1720—died 1769)

Pontiac was probably born near the Maumee River. Today this is in the state of Ohio. He was an Ottawa, but became the leader of several tribes.

He helped the tribes attack the English in 1763. The tribes wanted to drive the English out of the country. They wanted them to leave Michigan, Ohio and Pennsylvania. The Indians had very good plans of attack. They almost won. They attacked twelve forts, and only four of them held out. After much fighting, the tribes gave up, and they signed a peace treaty.

Pontiac was one of the greatest American Indians. He tried to do what he thought was best for his people. In 1769 he was murdered by an Indian from another tribe. He was near St. Louis, Missouri, when this happened.

THE REVOLUTIONARY WAR

Before many years had passed, the English colonies started a revolution. They wanted freedom from the English king. We were far from the colonies. English soldiers were here though. They were at Mackinac Island and Detroit. Soldiers at Detroit sent raids to Kentucky to attack the Americans. The English at Detroit paid Indians to bring back American scalps. The English leader, Hamilton, was responsible for this. This hair buying made the Americans hate the English from Detroit.

The English were using Detroit as their main post in the midwest. Soldiers and Indians friendly to the English left from Detroit to attack American settlements.

The Americans sent George Rogers Clark to stop these attacks. He was only a young man of twenty-six. A force of 127 men followed him from Virginia to Ohio and Indiana. They captured a fort in Ohio and one in Indiana. When Hamilton and the English heard of this, they marched south to stop Clark.

American soldiers raise the flag at Detroit.

The English took back their fort in Indiana. They did not, however, count on the bravery of the Americans. Clark and his soldiers returned. They had to make a difficult march in the middle of winter to do this. Once more they captured the fort. This time they captured Hamilton too. They took him prisoner for his crimes.

George Rogers Clark planned to go on to Detroit and take it also. There was a shortage of supplies though. The Americans tried to raise money for more supplies, but they could not. The American soldiers stayed in Ohio.

Even though the English kept Detroit, they lost much of their power. Clark and his men had done an important job. Their work helped to make Michigan and land northwest of the Ohio River a part of the United States. When the peace treaty was made with England, this land was turned over to the United States.

In 1783 the revolution was over; the colonies were free! The United States became a nation. But wait! The English were not leaving Michigan! They stayed in their forts. They traded for some furs with the tribes. They even sent guns and supplies to some tribes. The Americans became fed up with this. They sent General "Mad" Anthony Wayne to fight these tribes. He defeated them in 1794. Wayne County is named after the general.

The English were afraid more soldiers might be sent to attack them. In addition, the fur trade was not as important now. There were not many animals left. Finally, two years later, the English decided to give up Michigan. In 1796, Michigan was, at last, really a part of the United States.

Chapter Review:

In this chapter you should have learned these important things:
   a. who the Frenchmen, LaSalle, Marquette and Cadillac were
   b. where the French made their first settlements in Michigan
   c. why the French came to Michigan
   d. what things happened, after the French came, to change the lives of the Indians
   e. some of the useful things invented by the Indians
   f. why the French had to leave Michigan
   g. what Chief Pontiac did

QUESTIONS TO ANSWER

1. Why did the French come to Michigan? Give two reasons.

2. Who were the first Europeans to come? When did they come?

3. Where were the first French settlements in Michigan?

4. Tell how life changed for the tribes after the Europeans came.

5. Why did the tribes trade furs?

6. Why did the Europeans trade furs?

7. What things did the tribes leave for us today?

8. Name three important early French explorers.

9. Who started the city of Detroit?

(Questions continued on next page)

10. Name something that might be found in the ground which would tell us about the people long ago.

11. Why did the French lose power in Michigan?

12. When did the English come to Michigan?

13. What problem did the English cause the tribes?

14. Who was Pontiac, and what did he do?

15. Soldiers from which side were in Michigan during the Revolutionary War?

16. What caused the English to leave Michigan? When did this happen?

Words You Should Know

Here are words you should know before you read chapter 5.

baking powder
- canal
Finland
Germany
Holland
Italy
Ireland
- land office
- malaria
Massachusetts

- massacre (MASS-ah-ker)
mosquitoes
New Jersey
New York
plowed
Poland
prophet (PROF-it)
rattlesnakes
Russia
Shawnee (Sha-NEE)

shallow
Spain
stone fences
- surveyors
Sweden
Tecumseh (Ta-KUM-sah)
Tippecanoe
- townships
Vermont
White Pigeon
Windsor (WIN-zor)

Chapter 5

PIONEERS ARRIVE

Cutting trees to start a farm in the 1800's.

Americans have always wanted more elbow room. Men and women seem to want to have land around their homes, and not to have neighbors too close to them. Soon after the Revolutionary War was over, people started to move west. Many of them were after adventure, something new and exciting. Some people wanted to have a challenge.

They came from many places too. At first, most of the pioneers moved from states in the East. As time went on, more arrived from foreign countries. People moved to Michigan from places in Africa, Canada, England, Russia, Spain, Finland, Germany, Holland, Ireland, Italy, Poland and Sweden. It is a long list, and it does not stop here.

Land was cheap in the Michigan area. Most of it had not been farmed before. Land in the eastern states had been used for a long time. Farmers thought it was worn out. A chance for adventure and a chance to start a new farm brought most of the pioneers to Michigan.

Michigan was a long trip from the eastern states. There were no good roads or trains. The traveling was hard. Riding horseback or in a covered wagon were the ways most people came. Almost everyone coming west had to go through Ohio, so some people started farms there. Since Michigan was further away, many did not want to come here.

There were other reasons pioneers did not want to come. Early surveyors said most of the land was a swamp. It was only good for raising mosquitoes and rattlesnakes. This was not true. It did not make people excited though. The farmers also knew that almost all the land here was covered by forests. They would have to chop all the trees down before they could start a farm! If they did not get a crop planted soon enough, they would starve. These were some of the reasons why pioneers did not want to come at first. Some people did come though. They were brave and hardworking. The population grew slowly.

WAR OF 1812

Before Michigan had a chance to grow much, there was more trouble with the English. Michigan was still a territory, not yet a state. Detroit was a small city, but at that time it was the capital. Governor William Hull lived in Detroit as he was in

English soldiers land on Mackinac Island during the War of 1812.

charge of the Michigan Territory. American soldiers looked after the fort in Detroit. On the other side of the Detroit River was an English fort. This was called Fort Malden.

Many Americans thought Canada could be taken away from the English. Governor Hull, who had been made a general, and his soldiers crossed the Detroit River. They went into Windsor, Canada. They did not attack Fort Malden though. General Hull was not sure what to do. He waited for several days. He wanted to get his cannons across the river, and this took time.

Lewis Cass was with General Hull. He thought they should attack right away. Many soldiers were very upset with the General. Soon they started to run out of food. Then, more English soldiers marched to help those at Fort Malden. Other English soldiers took the American fort on Mackinac Island. This was upsetting to General Hull. He thought these English soldiers would come from the north now.

The men from Michigan went back to Detroit. General Hull was also very worried about Indians. There were many Indians with the English. General Hull was afraid Indians would attack people in and near Detroit. He would not have enough soldiers to protect everyone.

This time allowed the English to get ready, and their commander did decide to attack Detroit. First, the English cannons were fired. Cannon balls fell on the city. People were taken by surprise. Everyone ran right and left to take cover. One family was just starting to eat breakfast. A cannon ball fell through the roof. It smashed into the table and went into the basement. They were not hurt, but they left in a hurry!

Soon the English marched toward Detroit. General Hull had his cannon ready but did not shoot. He told his men to give up. They said they should fight! But English soldiers marched into Detroit and took the city without a shot being fired. People have always wondered if General Hull did the right thing. Lives were saved though.

Detroit was important, however, and the Americans were not going to give up so easily. Other American soldiers later marched from Kentucky to take Detroit back. They never quite made it. They were attacked at Monroe on the River Raisin. Over two thousand men were in the fight. It was a very bloody fight and many died. This was probably the biggest battle ever in our state. The Americans had to surrender this time. They were beaten.

The wounded Americans were left behind with two English doctors. The next day Indians attacked and murdered our soldiers. This really made the Americans mad. The English had promised to protect the wounded men. This was called the River Raisin Massacre.

In this war the English also had ships on Lake Erie. They helped bring supplies to their soldiers. Oliver Hazard Perry had been building American ships to fight the English.

A cannonball falls through the roof of a house in Detroit. War of 1812.

Soon the English ships and Perry's ships went to battle. This battle was in Lake Erie not too far from Detroit. The fight was bitter. There were six English ships and nine American ships. On Lieutenant Perry's ship, 83 of the 103 sailors were killed or wounded. He had to leave his ship as it was nearly wrecked. In spite of these losses, the Americans finally won.

Lieutenant Perry sent a message to those on shore. "We have met the enemy and they are ours. . . ."

The war was over in 1814. The English were beaten, and Michigan was free. The English left Detroit and Michigan for good.

TECUMSEH—INDIAN WARRIOR (born about 1768—died 1813)

Tecumseh was born in Ohio. His father was a Shawnee, and his mother came from the Creek tribe.

Tecumseh lived in a time of great change. During his life he saw European settlers taking away the tribes' land. The tribes were being overrun. When he became a man, he tried to stop this. He did not want settlers on Indian land.

Tecumseh's father and two of his brothers were killed in a battle to drive out the settlers. This was the Battle of Fallen Timbers in 1794. Some Indians decided to make peace after this, but not Tecumseh. He began to get other Indians to fight also.

These Indians decided to get help from the English. They wanted to use the English to get rid of the Americans. Many Americans were moving onto their land.

His brother, known as the Prophet, attacked the Americans in 1811. This was a famous battle called Tippecanoe. It was a hard fight, but the tribes lost. The American leader named William Harrison won. Later, Harrison became United States president.

The War of 1812 was between the English and the United States. Tecumseh joined the English soldiers. He and his men fought in Canada across from Detroit.

Tecumseh and the others were greatly feared by the Americans. One reason why Detroit surrendered was that the American leader there was afraid of the Indians.

Later, the English retreated. Tecumseh got the English to make a last fight against the Americans. It was during this battle, in Canada, that he was killed.

There is a city in southern Michigan named after Tecumseh.

50

TRAVELING TO THE NEW LAND

In the 1820's and 1830's some new ideas in travel started. There were now a few steamships. They could travel even when the wind did not blow. The Erie Canal was also opened. This was really important. Today, we do not talk much about canals. But they were once very valuable. A canal was like a man-made river. Small shallow boats could be pulled up and down the canal by horses. What a strange way to make a ship move! It did work though. This was not a fast way to travel, but it was not much work after getting started.

The Erie Canal went to Lake Erie from the Hudson River in New York state. Now it was possible to go all the way from New York to Detroit by boat. Goods could be sent back and forth. The farmers could ship leftover crops to the East to be sold. More and more pioneers used the Erie Canal and the Great Lakes to come to Michigan. Our population grew and grew. In 1820 we had 8,765 people in Michigan; by 1840 we had 212,267!

The Erie Canal.

STARTING THE FARMS

Most of the pioneers coming to Michigan were farmers. The cities were still small. There were no large factories where people could work. Before a farm could be started, land had to be bought. The men would find a good place to farm. Then they would go to a land office, such as the ones at Kalamazoo or White Pigeon. Each person would have to know where his land was located. This was not simple when woods and forests were everywhere.

51

A few years before, surveyors had set out on horseback. They traveled over the hills and through the swamps. Their job was to mark out lines going north and south, also east and west. These lines were used on maps so that the new farmers could find their land. The whole state was divided into make-believe squares called townships. These also made it easier to find land. Roads were later built on the township lines. This helped the farmers reach their land.

Using the lines the state had been divided into, each farmer explained where his land was to be. Most of the land belonged to the United States government. The price set for the land was at least $1.25 an acre. It was sometimes more.

Once a family reached its new land, all of the trees had to be cut down. It is hard to realize how many trees were here then. Almost the whole state was covered by them. The trees were either chopped down, burned down, or the bark cut off so they would die. If the trees stayed, the farmer could not.

Next, the ground had to be plowed. There were no tractors. A team of oxen or mules would be used. The farmer had to walk behind the plow and guide it. He could not go far before he ran into a tree stump or a large rock. It was hard work to get rid of these! The rocks were used to make fences. These stone fences can still be seen in some places today.

Many of the early pioneers in Michigan became sick. They were often very ill with chills and fever. They did not know what caused this disease. Today we do. It was malaria, carried by mosquitoes. There are very few cases of malaria in Michigan now. We have drugs to treat it, and we can control the mosquitoes.

BLACKSMITHS, STOREKEEPERS AND FISHERMEN

Of course there were people who did not farm. Blacksmiths were very important then. They fixed horseshoes and wagon wheels. Sometimes they helped to make barrels. Wooden barrels were used to ship many things.

Other people ran general stores. The general store had almost everything that could be bought. The farmers came to them for cloth or baking powder or nails—whatever they needed and could not make themselves. The general store often was the first post office too. To get a letter was exciting! It might be the only way a person would ever hear from his family or friends. Travel was expensive, and it took great effort and a long time.

Some of our pioneers went fishing. But this was not for fun! It was their work. They went out in the Great Lakes in small sailboats. They used nets to catch many kinds of fish. They sold the extra fish they did not need. The fish might have been

A general store. (Michigan State University Museum)

dried and mixed with salt or smoked in a smokehouse. Then they would be placed in barrels and shipped to the city, maybe Detroit. There were no iceboxes or refrigerators, but some people did have ice. Where did it come from? It came from Michigan lakes when they were frozen in the winter. The ice from the lakes was cut up into blocks. These were packed in sawdust until summer. What a way to get an ice cube!

Chapter Review:

In this chapter you should have learned these important things:
  a. that Tecumseh was an important Indian leader
  b. that Detroit was given up to the English in the War of 1812
  c. that the Battle of the River Raisin was one of the biggest in Michigan history
  d. that Oliver Hazard Perry's American ships won in a battle against English ships on Lake Erie
  e. that fishing was an important way of getting food in the early years

QUESTIONS TO ANSWER

1. Why did the pioneers want to come to Michigan?

2. Tell why some settlers did not want to come.

3. What country did we fight in the War of 1812?

4. In the War of 1812 two important places in Michigan were captured. One was Fort Mackinac. What was the other place?

5. There was a very big battle in Michigan during the War of 1812. After it was over, wounded soldiers were killed. What city was this battle near?

6. Oliver Hazard Perry fought the English in the War of 1812. Where did he do his fighting? Did he win?

7. What important improvements in travel helped early settlers reach Michigan?

8. What state is the Erie Canal in?

9. Between the years of 1820 and 1840 did the population grow very much?

10. How did most early settlers make a living?

11. The whole state is divided into little squares on some maps. The lines for the squares were made by surveyors. The squares can help to find where a certain piece of land is. What are the squares called?

12. What did a pioneer farmer have to do before the crops could be planted?

13. What insect caused early Michigan pioneers to become sick?

14. In pioneer times there was someone who did important work. We do not see or hear much about this person now. He also helped fix wagon wheels. Who was this person?

Words You Should Know

Here are words you should know before you read chapter 6.

- attorney general
  Cassopolis (Kah-SOP-a-lis)
- districts
- executive branch
- House
  Lansing
  legislative branch

  lieutenant governor
  Mason, Stevens T.
  Milliken
  Northwest Territory
- representatives
  Richard, Gabriel (Ree-SHARD)
  Romney

  Schoolcraft
- Senate
  senators
- Supreme Court
  Toledo
  Traverse City
  Tuscola (Tus-KO-la)
  Williams, G. Mennen

People in Michigan have their roots from many places. These girls are dancing a Scottish dance at Alma, Michigan. Each year there is a festival at Alma for people to remember the old Scottish customs.
(Travel Bureau—Michigan Dept. of Commerce)

55

Soldiers from Michigan march trying to keep the Toledo area for Michigan.

Chapter 6

ON THE ROAD TO STATEHOOD

In the early days Michigan was not a state. After the Revolutionary War, it was a part of the Northwest Territory. This territory later was divided into several states. Ohio, Wisconsin and Michigan were all in this first big territory. We were made into our own territory in 1805. This was the step before being a state. In 1805 we had a capital in Detroit. The United States government said we could become a state when we had 60,000 people living here. We could not vote in the House or Senate in Washington, D.C., until we were a state. In 1804 there were many territories waiting to become states. A territory was under the control of the United States government in many ways. The people living in them wanted to start states so they could have more control.

Ohio and Indiana became states, but Michigan was still a territory. Finally, we had enough people living here to form a state. Word was sent to the Congress in Washington, D.C. Congress said, "Not so fast." We had been arguing with Ohio over the little village where Toledo is today. It was supposed to be in Michigan, but Ohio thought it was theirs! This problem would have to be solved first.

THE TOLEDO WAR

Armed soldiers had been sent to Toledo to keep it for Michigan. There were a few fights, but no one was killed. President Jackson said this fighting must stop. It was finally suggested Michigan give up the Toledo area in a trade. Michigan would be given the western part of the Upper Peninsula. This land had not been a part of Michigan. Some people did not think it was a good deal. The land was far away and too cold. What could it be good for? Well, it was worth quite a bit. It had trees for lumber. It had copper and iron too! It was a very fair trade.

At long last, Congress let us become a state in 1837. This is the story of how we now have the two peninsulas as they are today!

THE BOY GOVERNOR

Stevens T. Mason was our first state governor. He was known as the Boy Governor since he was only twenty-three years old then. Mr. Mason led the state well. He was governor until 1840.

Stevens Mason   Lewis Cass   Father Richard

LEWIS CASS—A Man Who Helped Build Michigan (born 1782—died 1866)

Lewis Cass was born in New Hampshire. As a young man he moved with his family to Ohio. While he was there he studied law.

He became a soldier and fought in the War of 1812. He was one of the soldiers protecting Detroit when it was surrendered to the British. Cass was sure the British could have been beaten.

In 1813 he was made the governor of Michigan. Michigan was just a territory then. Only about 6,000 people who were not Indians lived here. He kept this job for eighteen years.

Cass left his mark on Michigan history. He suggested the state motto. He designed the state seal. He started the Historical Society of Michigan. Cass City and Cassopolis are cities that were named for him. There are also a county and a river with his name.

He was a strong and able leader. He did much for Michigan and his country.

FATHER GABRIEL RICHARD (Ree-SHARD)—The Priest of Detroit (born in France—died 1832 at Detroit)

Father Richard was a priest. He was almost beheaded in the French Revolution. This was a time of terror in France. Father Richard would not take an oath to be loyal to the new government. He escaped from France and came to America on a sailing ship.

He went to Illinois to work with the tribes. In 1798 he arrived in Detroit to become the priest at St. Anne's Church.

One morning in 1805 a terrible fire started. Before long, the town had burned down. Nothing was left. Father Richard pitched in to help. He gathered food and clothing for those who lost their homes. He was heard to say, "We hope for better things; it will arise from the ashes."

Many years later, these words were put into Detroit's city motto. The words are on the city seal.

58

HENRY SCHOOLCRAFT—Writer About Indian Tales (born 1793—died 1864)

Henry was born in Albany County, New York. He went with Lewis Cass to explore Michigan. He traveled with Cass around Lake Superior. They explored the Michigan copper country.

He became interested in the Indians and their life. In 1822 he was made the Indian agent for the tribes near Lake Superior. Henry married a Chippewa girl. From 1836 to 1841 he was in charge of Indian affairs for Michigan.

Schoolcraft listened to Indian tales and legends. He wrote them down and had them printed. Another writer named Longfellow read some of Schoolcraft's information. Longfellow used this to write the poem called *Song of Hiawatha*.

Henry Schoolcraft helped to name many counties in our state. Often he used Indian words and put them together in a new way. *Tuscola* is an example. This is from part of two Indian words and could mean "level land." It is the name of one of our counties.

Schoolcraft was an interesting man in our state's history. He helped to pass on to us the legends of the Indians. They might have been forgotten without his efforts.

The Capitol in Lansing.

MICHIGAN'S CAPITAL YESTERDAY AND TODAY

When we were a territory, the capital was in Detroit, the largest city. Detroit stayed the capital until 1847. Then it was moved to Lansing. At that time there was nothing much to Lansing. It was far from other cities and towns. Many people thought it was a joke to put the capital there. It was done because it was more in the middle of the state. Today, Lansing is a large city. The capital is still there. There are many factories and auto plants there too.

The first capitol building in Lansing is gone now. In 1879 a larger one was completed. If you visit the capitol, this is the one you will see. It has a large white dome. On one side of the building is the Michigan Senate. On the other side is the Michigan House of Representatives.

The House of Representatives and the Senate make the laws for our state. Michigan is divided into House and Senate districts. The people in each district vote for the representatives and senators who go to Lansing and make our laws.

THREE BRANCHES OF STATE GOVERNMENT

Our state government has three parts, known as branches. Each branch has certain duties. The legislative branch makes the laws. The House and Senate are in this branch. There is also a House and Senate in the United States Congress in Washington, D.C. The people in Michigan vote for senators and representatives to go to Washington, too.

The executive branch upholds the laws. The governor is a part of this branch. The State Police are too. There are other men in the executive branch. There is a lieutenant governor who helps the governor. We have an attorney general who is the lawyer for the state. There is a secretary of state. He manages many offices in Michigan. He is in charge of all drivers' licenses and the sale of car license plates. There are several other departments in the governor's branch. One of these is in charge of state highways; another looks after our natural resources. The Department of Education is a third.

The governor has many jobs. He must choose the people who will be in some of the state offices and members of state boards. For example, he says who will be the state treasurer. Choosing these people is one of the strongest of the governor's powers. He also has the say whether a law is passed. He can decide not to sign a bill to make it become a law. It can still pass if two-thirds of the members of the House and Senate vote for the law. This makes the governor a very powerful person in state government.

The governor has his office in the capitol building. The State Supreme Court was once there too. Now there is not enough room for all the offices in the capitol. Many new office buildings have been built in Lansing. The state government has grown a great deal.

The third branch is the one with our state courts. They decide the law. Judges say what the law is supposed to mean. The state Supreme Court is in this branch.

Now you should know that our government has three branches. You should also know what duty each branch has.

G. Mennen Williams   William G. Milliken

G. MENNEN WILLIAMS—A Michigan Governor and Judge (born 1911—   )

He was born in Detroit. His mother's family name was Mennen. Her family ran the Mennen Company which still makes soap and shaving cream. Ever since he was a boy he was called "Soapy" because of this. His first name is Gerhard. He did not like his name; so he never used it.

During World War II he was in the Navy. After the war was over, he became Governor of Michigan. He was well liked by the average person. He set a record by being elected to be governor six times.

He always wore a bow tie. This was a little unusual. His bow tie was green with white dots. G. Mennen Williams is well remembered by his bow tie!

In 1960 he became Secretary of State for African Affairs. Since 1970 G. Mennen Williams has been on the Michigan Supreme Court in Lansing.

WILLIAM G. MILLIKEN—A Calm and Steady Governor (born 1922—   )

William Milliken is from Traverse City. During World War II he flew on a bomber. He went on many missions and was given medals for his bravery. After the war ended, he went back to Traverse City. His family owns a department store there, and he helped to run it for awhile.

Bill Milliken went to Yale University. From 1960 to 1964 he was a state senator. Then he was elected lieutenant governor in 1964 and 1966.

George Romney was the governor of Michigan, but he left to take a job in Washington, D.C. So, in 1969, William Milliken became the governor of Michigan.

Governor Milliken has now been elected three times. By 1982 he will have been governor for fourteen years. This is the longest ever for a Michigan governor. G. Mennen Williams was elected more times, but the terms were only two years then.

Chapter Review:

In this chapter you should have learned these important things:
   a. that Lewis Cass, Father Richard and Henry Schoolcraft were three early Michigan pioneer leaders
   b. that Michigan was a territory before it was a state
   c. that there was almost a war between Michigan and Ohio over the land where Toledo is now located
   d. that Michigan was made a state in 1837
   e. that Stevens T. Mason was the first state governor
   f. where the first capital was located and where the capital is today
   g. who G. Mennen Williams and William G. Milliken are

QUESTIONS TO ANSWER

1. Who was Lewis Cass?

2. What problem kept Michigan from becoming a state for a while?

3. What happened so that the Upper Peninsula became a part of Michigan?

4. When did Michigan become a state?

5. Who was Stevens T. Mason?

6. Where was the first capital of Michigan?

7. Where is the capital today?

8. What are the three branches of our state government?

9. Which branch has two parts?

10. Name some things the governor does.

11. There is a House and Senate for the Michigan state government in Lansing. In what city is the House and Senate for the U.S. Congress located?

Words You Should Know

Here are words you should know before your read chapter 7.

Adrian
Albion
Ann Arbor
• assassinated
Battle Creek
Baumfree, Isabella
• bounty hunters
Bunche, Ralph
Civil War
Clinton

Coldwater
conductors
Confederacy
Crosswhite, Adam
Detroit
• infantry
Louisville
Marshall
Moore, Colonel
• Nobel Peace Prize

• political parties
Port Huron
• Republican Party
sheriff
• slavery
Sojourner Truth
Underground railroad
• Union
West Point Academy
Ypsilanti (Ip-si-LAN-tee)

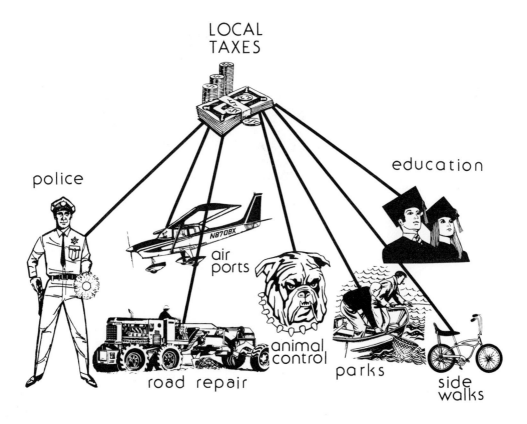

Your parents pay taxes to many units of government. This money is used in different ways. The picture in the chart show some of the ways it is used.

Escaping slaves passing through Michigan. Many people helped them on their way.

Chapter 7

ON THE WAY TO FREEDOM

The United States has always been famous as the home of the brave and the free. At first we were not really honest about this because we allowed slavery. Some people tried to have it outlawed. It was not easy. Many people thought it was all right. After far too many years, slavery was stopped. This was one of the reasons for the Civil War between the North and the South in the 1860's.

Michigan never allowed slavery; but a few people did have slaves in the early days. Many people in Michigan knew slavery was very wrong.

ADAM CROSSWHITE'S STORY

Adam Crosswhite and his family had escaped slavery. They had run away from Kentucky. Adam settled near Marshall, Michigan. He was respected in the town. But he was afraid slave hunters would come after him someday. He told his friends that he would fire his gun in the air as a signal if they tried to get him. His friends would then run to help him.

On a cold January morning they heard the warning shot! Four slave hunters and a deputy sheriff were at Adam's door! Soon there were so many people that the slave hunters were afraid they would be attacked. Adam and his family escaped on a train to Canada.

The people from Kentucky were very angry. They wanted the United States Congress to pass laws so they could catch their slaves! Congress did this. It was a bad time for the escaped slaves. People in Michigan passed other laws to keep the sheriff and police from helping slave hunters in Michigan.

Before the Civil War, there were many slaves in the southern states.

TWO WOMEN SPEAK OUT

A black woman from New York moved to Michigan. The city where she moved was Battle Creek. She called herself Sojourner Truth and spoke against slavery. One of her sons had been taken from her and sold. No wonder she was angry! She went to court and was able to have him freed. She decided to help other slaves too.

Sometimes these slaves escaped from their owners. Then they came north. Even after they reached the free states, it was not safe. Bounty hunters tried to catch them and take them back. It was against the law to help escaped slaves too!

Even so, Sojourner and others tried to help. They worked to find places for the slaves to hide. They had wagons pick them up and hide them inside—maybe under a load of straw. All of this was called the *Underground Railroad*. It was not a railroad. It was not underground either! It was a code name. Houses where slaves could hide were called stations. People who helped were called conductors.

Many of the escaped slaves came through Michigan. Most did not stay here. They went to Canada. In Canada they knew they were free. They were in another country, and could not be brought back!

Several towns in southern Michigan had Underground Railroad "stations." These were in Battle Creek, Coldwater, Adrian, Albion, Ann Arbor, Clinton, Detroit, Kalamazoo, Marshall, Port Huron and Ypsilanti.

Another brave lady worked with the Underground Railroad. Her name was Laura Haviland. She lived in Adrian. Slave owners put a price of $3000 on her if she could be stopped! It is believed that 40,000-100,000 slaves escaped through the secret railroad.

Sojourner Truth

Ralph Bunche

SOJOURNER TRUTH—A Leader To Freedom (born 1778—died 1883)

Her real name was Isabella Baumfree. She was born a slave in New York state. When she was nine years old she was sold with some sheep for $104.00. In 1810 she was sold once more. This time the owner said she could be free—some day. But she worked so hard he did not want to do this.

She grew up to be a tall woman with a deep voice. Finally she got her freedom. In 1827 New York passed a law, and slavery was now outlawed. She left New York because someone tried to sell one of her children as a slave.

She started to call herself Sojourner Truth. She traveled, preached and talked against slavery. Sojourner came to Battle Creek, Michigan. Here she worked with the Underground Railroad. She helped slaves escape to Canada.

Once she was asked to visit President Lincoln. She went to Washington and talked with him. There she told him about the troubles of the slaves. President Lincoln asked her to help work in hospitals in the south.

Sojourner finally came home to Battle Creek. She died there when she was about 105 years old.

RALPH BUNCHE—A Man For Peace (born 1904—died 1971)

Ralph Bunche was born in Detroit. He studied very hard and went to several colleges. He attended the University of California and Harvard. He also studied overseas. He went to London and South Africa. He was a very smart man. He worked with a famous author on a book about Blacks in America. Ralph Bunche also worked for the State Deparment and was an expert in many fields. He was one of the first Black people to have a top job there. Mr. Bunche helped start the United Nations in 1945. He worked in the United Nations after that.

In 1947 he helped solve the problems in starting Israel. Israel was a new country formed from older ones. There were many problems to be solved. There were often fights with words and with guns. One of the men he was working with was assassinated. This did not stop Mr. Bunche. He helped keep things under control. He became famous because of this work and was known around the world. He received the Nobel Peace Prize in 1950. He was the first Black to get the prize.

By 1967 he had been promoted. He was now the Under-Secretary General of the United Nations.

Ralph Bunche worked hard during his life to keep peace in the world. The people of Michigan should be proud of him.

Joe Louis (Michigan State Archives)

JOE LOUIS—The Brown Bomber (born 1914—died 1981)

His real name was Joe Louis Barrow. He was born on a farm in Alabama. His family moved to Detroit in 1926 when he was twelve.

In 1937 Joe Louis won the world's heavyweight boxing championship. He was called the "Brown Bomber" because he was black and so tough.

He was the pride of Detroit. Joe Louis kept his title for eleven years, fighting twenty-five times to defend it. This was a real record! In 1949 he retired undefeated.

Joe had earned much money as a fighter, but he also spent and gave away a great deal of it. He was in debt and needed money for taxes. He tried to make a comeback and fought two more fights, but lost. In 1952 he quit boxing.

Joe Louis will never be forgotten. Detroit named its new sports arena in his honor. This was done in 1978. The city could not have made a better choice. Joe Louis died April 11, 1981 and was buried in the Arlington Cemetery in Washington.

The Republican Party started with a large meeting in Jackson.

THE REPUBLICAN PARTY IS BORN HERE

During the 1850's the anger over slavery increased. New states were starting in the West. Some of these wanted to have slavery. This was a bad problem. In Washington, laws were sometimes passed that allowed this. People in the north were upset with their political parties.

Meetings were held to start a new party. A large meeting was held at Jackson, Michigan, and about fifteen hundred people came. They decided to form a new party against slavery. The party was called the Republican Party. The year was 1854. Later, Abraham Lincoln ran for United States president as a Republican.

Several states wished to leave the United States because they wanted to keep slavery. These states were in the South. In 1861 a Union fort was attacked by the South. (The North was called the Union, and the South was called the Confederacy.) The Civil War had started. Michigan fought with the Union side. During the war, about 90,000 Michigan men went to fight. Many were killed and many others died of diseases.

FROM MICHIGAN TO THE BATTLEFIELDS

No battles were fought in Michigan, but we did have some famous people in the war. General George Armstrong Custer was from Monroe. Custer was not a general when the war started. He had just left West Point Academy. He was in the first battle of the war. Later, he went up in large balloons to see what the enemy was doing. Very few men wanted to do this! He also led daring raids into the enemy area. It was not long before he was made a captain.

Sometimes he led Michigan soldiers. He was always very bold, and he often shouted, "Come on you Wolverines!" to get his men to follow after him.

During the war he had at least ten horses shot from under him. Because he was a brave leader, he was made a general. He was one of the youngest ever! This surprised many of the older, more careful soldiers.

Custer is well known because he led troops against Indians in the West. He and all his men were killed at the Battle of the Little Big Horn in 1876.

George Custer (Michigan State Archives)

Sara Emma Edmonds

General Custer's fighting was exciting, but the story of another soldier is more unusual. Sara Emma Edmonds joined the Second Michigan Regiment. But wait! She was a woman. There were no women in the army in 1861! She pretended to be a man! Later, she joined the Secret Service as a spy. Sara went into the South behind enemy lines. In order to do this, she pretended to be a Black boy, a slave, an Irish woman and a southern soldier! Not all at the same time, of course.

Michigan soldiers fought in many battles. One of these was at Louisville, Kentucky. Here a few hundred men in the Michigan 25th Infantry stopped about three thousand soldiers from the South! The southern army wanted to capture Louisville. But the Union commander, Colonel Moore, knew he had to win. His men were the only ones there to do the job. He did such a good job leading the soldiers, the southern leader said Moore should be made a general for his skill! And he was.

The Civil War was very bloody. When it was over, the soldiers came home. Many Michigan men had died to save the union. Those who were left tried to forget the battles; instead they tried to look to the future. They went back to work on their farms, in the stores, offices and factories. There was much to do in Michigan because our state was growing. There were homes and factories to build, and there were the farms and new industries where people could work.

Chapter Review:

In this chapter you should have learned these important things:
a. that escaped slaves came through Michigan to get to Canada
b. what the Underground Railroad was
c. who Sojourner Truth, Ralph Bunche and Joe Louis were
d. what happened to Adam Crosswhite
e. that the Republican Party was started in Michigan
f. that Michigan was on the Union (North) side in the Civil War
g. that General Custer was from Monroe, Michigan

QUESTIONS TO ANSWER

1. Who was Adam Crosswhite and what happened to him?

2. What did the Underground Railroad do?

3. Who was Sojourner Truth?

4. Who was Laura Haviland?

5. The Republican Party was started in which Michigan city?

6. Which Michigan city was the home of General George Armstrong Custer?

7. What made General Custer famous?

8. What did Sara Emma Edmonds do in the Civil War?

Words You Should Know

Here are words you should know before you read chapter 8.

Alpena (Al-PEE-na)
• assembly line
Central
Cheboygan (Shi-BOY-gan)
• cholera (KOL-er-a)
• compass
copper rush
Durant, William Crapo
• dynamite
East Norway
Escanaba (Es-ka-NAW-ba)
Fayette (FAY-et)

ghost town
Grand Rapids
horseless carriages
Hudson
• lock (Soo Locks)
• log jam
lumberjacks
Maxwell
Michigammee
Michiganian or Michigander
mining
narrow guage

Negaunee (Ni-GAW-nee)
Oakland
Oldsmobile
Overpack, Silas
• rapids
Reo (REE-o)
river hogs
scythes (SI-ths)
• shanty boys
ton
Victoria

Chapter 8

THE WAY OUR FOREFATHERS MADE THEIR LIVING

MINING COPPER—ONE OF NATURE'S RICHES

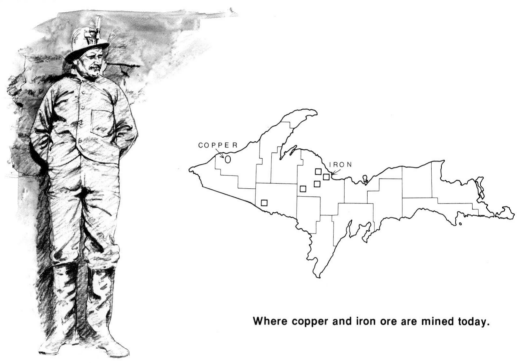

Where copper and iron ore are mined today.

Mining copper has been an important industry for Michigan. There have been many mines in the western part of the Upper Peninsula. This is where most of our copper is found.

Before the time of written history, the tribes mined copper too. This copper was taken from Isle Royale. Small pits show where the metal was removed. The copper on the island is pure and it is found in the cracks of rocks. The Indians broke the rocks with fire and cold water. The copper was used for spear points and arrowheads. Sometimes it was traded to other tribes. Pieces of Michigan copper have been found buried at old Indian villages far from our state. The tribes on Isle Royale were our first copper miners.

After awhile, the tribes left Isle Royale, and the copper was forgotten. Douglass Houghton was a famous Michiganian. He wrote reports about the copper here. He had traveled all over the state looking for valuable minerals, such as copper. He also told where different kinds of plants and trees grew. The Michigan government sent him to do these things. This was a new state, and people were trying to find out all about it.

In 1843 miners started going to the Upper Peninsula to find the copper. Soon, more and more miners arrived. It was a Michigan copper rush! Some of these men found copper. Some did not.

If copper was found, it was hard to move. Detroit was over five hundred miles away. The copper had to go by ship, passing first through Lake Superior. At Sault Ste. Marie it had to be unloaded. This was necessary because of the swift rapids there. The boats couldn't get through. The metal was reloaded into other boats and sent to Detroit to be melted and made into useful things. By 1849 many miners had left. Some went to California to the gold rush there. But over the years, much more money was made from Michigan copper than from California gold!

IRON: THE BACKBONE OF INDUSTRY

Iron ore was found in Michigan soon after copper. Iron is the backbone of industry. It is used to make steel. It is used for tall buildings, for cars, for knives and forks, for nails and even thumbtacks.

A man named William Burt had traveled to the Upper Peninsula. He was surveying the new state of Michigan. He was trying to make good maps. For his work it was important to use a compass. He needed to know which way was north and which was south. But his compass needle did not point north at all! His men found it was pointing toward large pieces of iron ore instead!

Some men from Jackson, Michigan, started a company to mine the iron. They went north and were guided to the iron ore by a Chippewa chief. They were amazed to find a mountain of iron ore. It was 150 feet high! They started the Jackson Mine near Negaunee. Today our iron mines are still in this area. They are in the western Upper Peninsula.

THE SOO LOCKS

People knew if a canal and locks could be built at Sault Ste. Marie, it would help shipping. It would help copper mining also. If it could be done, ships could sail in and out of Lake Superior. Lake Superior is twenty-one feet higher than the other Great Lakes. A lock would hold water and raise or lower ships coming and going.

Building the locks would be a great challenge. They were started in 1853. Charles Harvey was the man in charge of the work. Sixteen hundred men came to work on them. Sault Ste. Marie was a very long way from other cities. Almost

Michigan miners about 1880.

everyone had to come by ship. In the winter the temperature was sometimes thirty degrees below zero. The next year disease hit. It was cholera and this killed many of the men.

The locks were slowly being finished. There were two locks, and each was 350 feet long and 70 feet wide. When all the work was finally done, it cost almost one million dollars. This was a great deal of money for those days. The locks were finished in 1855.

Many ships started to use the locks. By 1875 over one million tons of goods went through every year.

With the help of the Soo Locks, copper mining increased. Large mines were opened. They went deep into the ground. Each year more copper was brought out. The most copper mined in one year was 270 million pounds. That is an amazing amount!

The Soo Locks at Sault Ste. Marie, Michigan. You can see that the ship in this old picture is much higher than the lower level. (Michigan State Archives)

WE HAVE GHOST TOWNS TOO!

Have you ever heard about ghost towns in Michigan? Of course, there are no ghosts there. These towns are places where the people have all left. Only the old homes and stores remain. Usually they are falling down. Sometimes there is not much left at all!

These old towns were near some of the copper and iron mines. When much mining was done, they were full of people. Some of the mines closed and, after a while, the people moved on to new jobs. Here are the names of a few of these towns: Central, Victoria, Michigamme, East Norway and Fayette. A few people have moved back to these towns. I wonder if they ever do see a ghost?

CUTTING DOWN THE GIANT TREES

You know that long ago Michigan was covered with trees. The first farmers cut down the trees to clear the land. They used some of the trees to build cabins. The trees gave them their bridges and barns too. They made furniture and butter churns from them. There were so many trees they were not worth very much.

As our nation began to grow, there was a greater need for lumber. More people moved to the western states. There are not as many trees there. They needed to have lumber sent to them by train. The demand for wood grew too. Sawmills were built in Michigan. Each year there were more trees cut than before.

The best tree for lumber was the White Pine. The pines grew in the Upper Peninsula and in the upper part of the Lower Peninsula.

Men were sent to the woods to see what land to buy. Large lumber companies bought the land and the trees. The trees were cut with axes and hand saws. The saws were big and they needed two men to work them.

The men who did all of the cutting and chopping were called lumberjacks or shanty boys. They were known as shanty boys because they lived in shanties or little bunkhouses. All of the men lived in the lumber camp.

At first, the work had to be done in the winter. There were several reasons for this. It was hard to move the big logs after the trees were cut down. To make it easier they were put on sleighs or dragged over roads covered with ice. Since the logs would float, rivers were used to move them to the sawmills. The logs were stacked up next to the river. The stack grew each day until spring. After the ice melted, the rivers were high with water. Then they flowed their fastest. All at once the logs were pushed into the river. Away they went! The lumbermen went along with them. Some men wore spiked boots and called themselves river hogs. It was their job to keep the logs from piling up into a log jam. If they did, the whole river would fill with logs. Sometimes dynamite was used to break up the jam! The work was dangerous and men lost their lives.

Paul Bunyan, the super lumberjack.

The brave lumberjacks often told stories in the bunkhouse at night. Each time the story was told, something was added to it. Soon, the stories were hard to believe, but that just made them better. One story was about a super lumberjack. His name was Paul Bunyan. Lumberjacks were big and strong, but Paul Bunyan was bigger and stronger! He had a pet ox called Babe. Babe was bigger than the whole lumber camp. Paul found Babe frozen in the ice of Lake Superior. He had turned blue from the cold! When it was time to move the lumber camp, Paul would build a raft of logs. Then he would lift the buildings and put them all on it. Next, Babe, the blue ox, was hitched to the raft. Off they went! They straightened out the roads as they traveled! It was said Paul Bunyan could cut down an acre of trees with one swing of his ax, or was it two acres!

A lumberjack with a log turning tool and a set of big wheels.

THE TREES KEEP FALLING

As time passed, the lumbermen discovered new ways to move the logs. A wagon maker named Silas Overpack from Manistee started to make big wheels. These were really BIG wheels! They were ten feet across. Two of them weighed about 2400 pounds. Logs were chained to an axle in the middle of two big wheels. Now horses or oxen could drag the logs. They could be moved in the summer or winter.

The lumberjacks moved up the rivers. They cut more and more trees. Before long, they could not find enough trees near the big rivers. They wanted to go deeper into the woods. A young man had the answer. He decided to build small railroads. These were called narrow-gauge because the tracks were narrow. The idea worked. Now, more trees were cut than ever before. There were many sawmills in towns such as Saginaw, Bay City, Muskegon, Manistee, Alpena, Cheboygan and Traverse City. After awhile, sawmills were built in the Upper Peninsula. More loggers went north. Menominee, Escanaba, Manistique and Baraga all had mills.

How much lumber came from Michigan? This was big business from 1840 to 1900. In these years people believe about 170,000,000,000 board feet were cut. That is enough wood to cover Michigan and Rhode Island with boards! It is more than can be even dreamed of!

Today we do not see so many trees here. The lumberjacks did not think about planting more trees. It took nature a long time to grow a state full of trees! The trees that were cut down were sometimes 150 feet tall. Now there are very, very few like that left. It will take time for the giant trees to grow back. We will all have to help them grow. This means everyone should be careful in the woods. We should not cut growing trees down. We should not leave camp fires burning. Forest fires can kill all the trees once again!

HARD WORK BEHIND THE PLOW

Many of the lumbermen went back to their farms in the summer. Most of the people in Michigan made their living on the farms then.

This was the time of real horse power. Horses were used to pull plows. They were used to pull wagons and carriages. Sometimes they were made to walk in circles and help machines work. They might power a small flour mill. Mules and oxen were used on the farms too.

The early farmers had few machines to help them. The wheat was cut by hand. The farmers walked through the fields with large cutters which they would swing to cut the grain. These cutters were called scythes (si-ths). Once the wheat was cut, the grain had to be taken from the stem. To do this, the wheat was laid on the ground. Then it was beaten with a stick or a flail. Next, it would be tossed into the air. The wind would blow the stems away and the grain would fall to the ground. It was swept up and put into bags. Now the farmer would take it to the mill to be ground into flour. The stems would be used as straw for the animals.

Early farmers with their scythes.

Most flour mills were next to a river or stream. They used water power to make the machinery work. Inside, the grain was ground between two large stones. The stones were round. They moved in circles to crush the grain. Flour came out the bottom.

81

Often the farmer gave part of the flour to the man who had the mill for doing the work.

Life on the farm was hard. There was always work to do. Children would say they did not have much time to play. They had to help their parents almost all the time.

HORSELESS CARRIAGE

Even people in the cities depended on the horse. Almost everyone had a stable. Each family had its own wagon or carriage. The horses had to be fed and kept clean. It was a good bit of trouble to have a horse and carriage.

About the year 1900, several people had ideas for an easier way to travel. They started to build horseless carriages. Of course, something had to make the carriage go. These people used small gasoline engines. Some even tried to use little steam engines.

When one of these inventors made his horseless carriage work, he would go for a drive. He, and perhaps a friend, would go up and down the city streets. Crowds would stop to watch. The horseless carriages were loud. They scared the horses. The horses would jump or run away! The men and women watching thought they would not replace the horse. The horseless carriage would be just a dream—a toy.

Three Michigan men did more than dream about a real horseless carriage. These men were Henry Ford, Billy Durant and Ransom Olds. They all tried to make a car that would run well. They each started a company to make cars. Billy Durant was already famous for making carriages. He had a factory to make carriages in Flint. He felt the horseless carriage would be the thing of the future though. The company Billy Durant started is now called General Motors. It is one of the biggest companies in the world. It still has factories in Flint.

Ransom Olds had a factory at Lansing. He made small cars there. He made a car called the "Curved-dash Olds." The year was 1900. This car was so popular songs were written about it! In 1903 one of his cars cost $650.00.

Henry Ford made a car in his garage. He was so excited he built it bigger than the door! He had to knock down part of the wall to get it out.

Ford worked for Thomas Edison in one of his power plants in Detroit. He left his job and started a car company; it failed. Later, a new company was started. His first cars were not very popular because they were quite expensive. In 1908 a new model was made. It was called the *Model T*.

82

OLDSMOBILE CURVED DASH RUNABOUT
BUILT FROM 1900 THROUGH 1904

SPECIFICATIONS

CAPACITY -- Two passengers.
WHEEL BASE -- 66 inches.
TREAD -- 55 inches.
FRAME -- Angle steel.
SPRINGS -- Oldsmobile side springs.
WHEELS -- 28-inch wood artillery.
TIRES -- 3-inch detachable.
MOTOR -- 5 x 6-inch 7 H. P. horizontal.
TRANSMISSION -- All-spur gear, two speeds
    forward and reverse.
FINISH -- Black with red trimming.

EQUIPMENT -- Complete set of tools and
    pair of large brass side lamps.
RADIATOR -- Copper disk.
CARBURETOR -- Oldsmobile.
IGNITION -- Jump spark.
STEERING GEAR -- Tiller.
DIFFERENTIAL -- Bevel-gear type.
BRAKES -- Differential and rear wheel.
WATER CAPACITY -- Five gallons.
CIRCULATION -- Gear pump.
GASOLINE CAPACITY -- Five gallons.

Henry Ford and Thomas Edison. Mr. Ford is on the left. (Michigan State Archives)

HENRY FORD—A Man With New Ideas (born 1863—died 1947)

Henry Ford was born on a farm close to Dearborn, Michigan. His mother died when he was twelve. He worked on the farm in the summer. He went to a one room school for his education.

Henry loved to repair things. He liked to work with clocks and watches, not even asking to be paid. He just loved to make something work again.

When he was sixteen, he went to work in Detroit as a mechanic. In 1884 he was married. To earn more money, Henry worked at night for the Detroit Edison Company. This company was started by Thomas Edison to make electricity. Henry Ford and Thomas Edison became good friends.

Henry Ford heard about gasoline engines and horseless carriages. He made his own gasoline engine in the kitchen! In 1896 he made a car in his workshop. It had wheels like those on a bicycle. In 1903 he and some others started the Ford Motor Company.

During his life he did many useful things. He helped start the moving assembly line for factories. He raised workers' wages much higher than they were before. His factories made things to help win World War I and II. He gave money to George Washington Carver. Mr. Carver did research on the uses of peanuts and other plants.

Henry Ford and others made some of the early all-metal airplanes. These were the first ones to carry passengers on regular airlines. Greenfield Village and Henry Ford Museum were started by him so we would all learn more about history. The list of things he did is long and he gave much to us all!

WILLIAM CRAPO DURANT—The Man Who Started General Motors (born 1871—died 1947)

William (or Billy) Durant was born in Boston. He moved to be with his grandparents in Flint, Michigan, in 1872.

When he was a young man he had a new idea for a buggy or carriage. He started his own company in 1886. It was not long before he had the largest carriage company in the world. Flint was known as the city that put the world on wheels—carriage wheels.

He felt, however, the car would be the way to travel in the future. In 1903, he started making cars too. He, and the men who helped him, started buying other auto companies. One of these was the Buick Company. In 1908 Durant started the General Motors Company. General Motors was made up of many smaller companies. Most of them made cars, but some of these companies made parts for cars.

It was not easy to start such a large company. Often it was hard to get enough money to run it. Banks thought making cars was a poor risk. They wanted to run the company if they loaned it money. Billy Durant had to fight several times to stay in control.

Mr. Durant was not a greedy man. He tried to protect the average person who had stock in his company. In 1929 the stock market went down. They say it "crashed." He tried to keep General Motors stock from falling too. He kept using his money to buy it. But he could not buy enough to keep the price up, and it fell too. Soon all the money he had saved was gone. He had lost millions of dollars. Later, another man took over the company.

Near the end of his life, Billy Durant ran a bowling alley in Flint. Many people had forgotten who he was. Billy Durant, however, had really put the world on wheels!

AN EARLY CAR

The first cars made plenty of noise and often scared horses.

The *Model T* was a very simple car. If anything went wrong, almost anyone could fix it. It was made in only one color—black. Some people called it the "Tin Lizzie." The car was cheap. It was made on an assembly line.

The assembly line was not really a new idea. But Henry Ford was the first to use it in such a big way. The assembly line carried the car frame along. It went slowly by each worker. Each person did his job, and the car then went on to the next man. Cars could be put together much faster this way. The price came down and more cars were sold.

Henry Ford made the *Model T* from 1908 to 1927. Over fifteen million were sold. More of these cars have been sold than any other kind, except the *Volkswagen Beetle!*

Many, many people worked in the car factories. The wages in most of these plants were very good. In 1914, Henry Ford raised the wages of each worker to five dollars a day. This does not seem like much money now, but it was about twice what the workers were paid then!

Most of the car factories are near Flint and Detroit today. Years ago there were factories in other cities. They made cars that we do not even hear about anymore.

They made cars called the *Hudson*, the *Maxwell*, the *Oakland* and the *Reo*, as well as many other kinds. After a while, these companies went out of business. Today, many factories across the state still make parts for cars though.

FURNITURE MAKING

Grand Rapids is the furniture capital of Michigan. People make furniture here. Today much office furniture is produced. Chairs and filing cabinets are made of wood and metal. In years past, furniture for the home was made also. It was made of Michigan wood. In 1880 over two thousand people made furniture in Grand Rapids. There were fifteen different companies for making furniture. Furniture from Grand Rapids was shipped by train all over the United States. Grand Rapids furniture is still well known for quality. The men and women who make this furniture are proud of their work.

A man making furniture in Grand Rapids. (Michigan State Archives)

Chapter Review:

In this chapter you should have learned these important things:

a. that some of the interesting industries of Michigan are copper and iron mining, lumbering, farming, the making of cars and furniture
b. that farming was our state's first big business
c. that copper was discovered in the 1840's
d. that the Soo Locks were built to get the copper and iron from Lake Superior
e. that the locks are needed because Lake Superior is a little higher than Lake Huron
f. that the car industry, our biggest today, started about 1900
g. who the three men were who helped start the car business

QUESTIONS TO ANSWER

1. Who were the very first miners?

2. Where was copper found in Michigan?

3. What did Douglass Houghton do?

4. How was iron discovered in Michigan?

5. Where is iron mined?

6. Why are there several ghost towns in Michigan?

7. What kind of tree was used so much during our days of lumbering?

8. Why were the rivers important to early lumbering?

9. Who was Paul Bunyan?

10. What was the *Model T?*

11. Where did R. E. Olds have his factory?

12. Who started the General Motors Company?

13. For what product was Flint famous before the invention of the car?

14. What city is the furniture capital of Michigan?

Words You Should Know

Here are words you should know before you read chapter 9.

alewife (AIL-wife)
- bulk
- Coho Salmon (Co-ho SA-mon)
- dolomite
- freighters
Frankfort
Grand Haven
- gypsum

herring
Holland
lighthouse
Ludington
pilothouse
Port Inland
- ports
radar

River Rouge
St. Clair
sea lamprey (LAM-pree)
steamship
Stoneport
trout
walleye
whitefish

This young skier is enjoying Michigan in the winter. Winter activities are an important part of our tourist industry. (Travel Bureau—Michigan Dept. of Commerce)

The Griffin built by LaSalle in 1679. The griffin is a make-believe animal that is half bird and half lion. There is a griffin on the front of the ship.

Chapter 9

THREE SIDES ON THE WATER: WE'RE A PENINSULA

SHIPPING

Before highways and roads were built, travel by land was hard. It was easier to follow nature's highways of water. These were the lakes and rivers in and around Michigan. The Indians used their canoes to go from place to place. The first Frenchmen used canoes to carry furs back to their forts.

In 1679 LaSalle decided to build a sailing ship. This ship was called the *Griffin*. It was the first sailing ship on the Great Lakes, except for Lake Ontario. The *Griffin* was built near Niagara Falls. LaSalle wanted to fill it with furs. It was a hard job to build such a big ship. Everything was made on the spot. Trees were cut and sawed. The boards were put together. The mast and sails were made.

Finally, the ship was finished. LaSalle and his men sailed across Lake Erie. They sailed to Mackinac and then they went on to Lake Michigan. The *Griffin* then put down its anchor on the Wisconsin shore. The furs were collected and put on board. LaSalle and a few men did not return with the *Griffin*. They took canoes and went to the St. Joseph River. Here they built a fort, which they called Fort Miami. It was named this because of the Miami tribe who lived there. This fort was where St. Joseph, Michigan, is today.

The *Griffin* was to sail back for LaSalle and his men. Spring came, but the *Griffin* did not come back. LaSalle was worried. What had happened to his ship? He did not have many supplies left; so he decided to walk back. He and his men walked all the way across the Lower Peninsula. LaSalle was the first European to see this part of Michigan. They finally reached a fort on Lake Ontario. No one knew about the *Griffin* there. It had disappeared. No one has ever found what happened to the *Griffin*—the first sailing ship on the upper Great Lakes. Did the *Griffin* sink in a storm? Did Indians attack it? Could it have become lost? No one knows!

As people moved to Michigan, more ships were built. At first these all used the wind for power. They were sailing ships like the *Griffin*. They helped bring pioneers. They carried cargo and they brought other things the pioneers needed.

In the 1800's, a new kind of ship was built. These ships used steam engines. They did not have to wait for the wind to blow.

The first steamship on the Great Lakes was called the *Walk-in-the-Water*. It used paddle wheels on the side to move it. Indians who saw it did not understand how it worked. Sometimes they said a great fish must pull it. The *Walk-in-the-Water* went across Lake Erie. It brought people to Detroit from Buffalo, New York. It took five days for the trip.

The *Walk-in-the-Water* made its trips for three years. In November, 1821, a storm came. The waves sent water rushing over the side. It was going to sink. The captain aimed the boat at the shore. He let it go onto the sand. The passengers were saved but it was a cold and scary ride!

More steamships were built for the Great lakes. They went between many cities. Some went to Chicago. Some went to Detroit or Marquette. Some went to Cleveland. Many people traveled by ship then. Sometimes the passenger ships would have races. It was very exciting to be on a ship during a race.

In the 1870's and 1880's, another new kind of ship was built. This ship was built just for the Great Lakes. It was used to carry cargo. This ship was long and low. It usually had a pilothouse for the captain. This was in front. The engine room was in the back with its smokestack. In the middle was the cargo. These ships carried iron ore, copper, coal, limestone, grain and lumber on the lakes. You can still see this kind of ship today. Now they are much bigger. They can be a thousand feet long!

One of these big freighters was the *Edmund G. Fitzgerald*. It was built at River Rouge, Michigan. When it was built, it was the largest ship on the Great Lakes. Today this ship is famous because of an accident. In November, 1975, it sank. It was carrying iron ore going to the Soo Locks. There was a terrible storm on Lake Superior. The ship broke in half and no one survived. It went to the bottom of the icy water. Gordon Lightfoot recorded a song about the *Edmund G. Fitzgerald*. It was a very sad thing to happen; twenty-nine men were killed. Of course, other ships have gone down on the Great Lakes. But this was a modern ship with radios, radar and lifeboats. It proves the Great Lakes can be dangerous. Even modern ships may not be a match for the Great Lakes—sometimes.

LIGHTHOUSES PROTECT OUR SHIPS

Sailors have always had to be careful. Today ships use radio to keep in touch. They use radar to know where other ships, islands and rocks are located. Years ago, sailors looked for lights on the shore. The lights warned them not to get too close. The light came from lighthouses.

The Edmund Fitzgerald caught in a storm on Lake Superior.

Men had to live at the lighthouses. They kept the light going at night and when there was fog. Sometimes they had a fog horn too. If a fog was too thick, sailors could not see a light. The sound would warn them.

The lighthouse at Point Betsie. (Travel Bureau—Michigan Dept. of Commerce)

You can still see lighthouses in Michigan, but most of them are closed now. Some are very old. There is a lighthouse at Point Betsie. This is near Frankfort on Lake Michigan. Another is near the Mackinac Bridge. One lighthouse is built on a rock three miles from land. It is the Rock of Ages Lighthouse near Isle Royale.

THE SOO LOCKS TODAY

The Soo Locks at Sault Ste. Marie are still important. Without the locks, ships could not leave Lake Superior. There is a rapids between Lake Superior and Lake Huron. New and bigger locks have been built. The locks had to grow because the ships kept getting larger. They are wider and longer now. The newest lock is 1200 feet long, 110 feet wide and 50 feet deep. It was built in 1968.

About 13,000 ships go through the locks each year. This is more than go through any other locks in the world!

OUR PORT CITIES

There are many Michigan ports on the Great Lakes. Ports are places where ships stop to pick up or unload cargo.

94

An ore ship passing Detroit. (photo by Harry J. Wolf)

Detroit is the Michigan port with the most cargo shipped. If you visit Detroit, go to the waterfront. You can watch the huge ships on the Detroit River.

Some ships are just passing through. They are on their way to other ports. Many of the ships are not from the Great Lakes. They are from across the oceans. Ships from England, Japan, and even Russia, travel to the Great Lakes. They use the St. Lawrence Seaway. The Seaway lets them come from the Atlantic Ocean and pass around Niagara Falls. The Seaway was built in 1959. It lets the large ships into the Great Lakes. All of these ships going into Lake Huron, Lake Michigan or Lake Superior pass by Detroit.

If you watch these ships, you may see a ship going to Chicago, Escanaba, or Muskegon. The ships on the Lakes carry many cargoes. About a third of the ships will have iron ore. Limestone and cement are often carried too. These are bulk cargoes. The bulk cargoes are ones that can be poured into the hold of the ship. The long, low Great Lakes freighters carry the bulk cargoes. Some ships also carry coal to power plants. The oceangoing ships may have cars for overseas. They may have wheat for India or cargoes for countries anywhere in the world.

At Marquette, iron ore is loaded into ships. At Port Dolomite and Drummond Island dolomite rock is loaded. Port Gypsum sends gypsum rock to make cement. Other Michigan ports are St. Clair, Alpena, Stoneport, Port Inland, Frankfort, Manistee, Ludington, Muskegon, Grand Haven and Holland.

The Great Lakes are still a highway to bring and send cargo. Paper made in Canada comes by ship to Michigan. Cars and trucks from Michigan go across the Atlantic in ships. Trains also go across the Great Lakes. Since they do not float, they are loaded into ships too. They are sent to Wisconsin, Canada and the Upper Peninsula this way. People were once able to put their cars on ships to cross Lake Michigan. That way they did not have to drive around the lake.

FISHING THE COLD WATERS

The Great Lakes are very important to us. We do more than travel over them though. We eat fish from the Great Lakes too.

People have fished in the Great Lakes from the earliest times. The tribes fished there. The explorers fished, and so did the pioneers. The pioneers ate the fresh fish. They also dried the fish. They added salt to the fish and this kept the fish from spoiling.

More fishermen came to the Great Lakes. They used nets and special boats to catch the fish. Each year more fish were caught. Whitefish, herring, trout and walleye came from the lakes. By 1900, over 100 million pounds of fish had been caught. The Great Lakes fish were food for many people.

Today the fishing is not so important. Almost as many fish are caught, but they are not as good to eat. They are not the same kinds anymore.

We took too many fish from the lakes. Some kinds are rare now. We did not treat the water very well. Chemicals were dumped in. Waste and garbage were added. These things hurt the fish. They also hurt people who eat the fish. Some kinds of fish are not healthy to eat now because the fish have chemicals in them.

A new creature got into the Great Lakes. This was the sea lamprey (LAM-pree). It has a sucking mouth with sharp teeth, and it looks like an eel. The lamprey came from the ocean. They held onto the bottoms of ships. When canals were built for ships, the lamprey went along. This is how they got into the lakes around Michigan. The lamprey sucks blood from fish. It can kill the fish or make it very weak. In this way the lamprey helped to kill fish in the Great Lakes.

After awhile, there were not many big fish left. A little fish moved in. It is called the alewife. It is not good to eat. They are used for pet food. If there had been enough large fish, they would have eaten all the alewives. Sometimes eighty percent of the fish caught are alewives. Once in a while the alewives die suddenly. So many can die at one time that the beaches are covered with dead fish. This makes it no fun to go swimming.

To help stop the lamprey we have used special chemicals. The chemicals go into the streams and they kill the baby lamprey. This is a good use of chemicals.

New fish have been put into the Great Lakes. The new fish are Coho Salmon. The salmon are doing well. Men have done this so there will be a better kind of fish to catch. There are not as many alewives now. If we are lucky, the Great Lakes will give us more fish to eat. There may be enough to feed many people once again.

Remember the Great Lakes are very important to our state. Ships use the lakes; fish come from the lakes. The Great Lakes give us places to swim in the summer. Cool winds come from the lakes when it is hot. They also give us water to drink. We must be careful with the lakes and should be thankful for them.

A Sea Lamprey on a fish. (Michigan D.N.R.)

97

Chapter Review:

In this chapter you should have learned these important things:

   a. that the Griffin was the first sailing ship on the Great Lakes (other than Lake Ontario)

   b. who built the Griffin and what happened to it

   c. that the first steam-powered ship to stop at Detroit was Walk-in-the-Water

   d. what happened to the modern freighter, Edmund G. Fitzgerald

   e. the St. Lawrence Seaway lets ships from the ocean reach Michigan

   f. that Detroit is the biggest port in Michigan

   g. that the sea lamprey and chemicals dumped in the Great Lakes have hurt the fishing business

QUESTIONS TO ANSWER

1. What was the *Griffin?* Who built it?
2. What was special about the ship, *Walk-in-the-Water?*
3. What happened to the freighter, the *Edmund G. Fitzgerald?*
4. Draw a small picture of a Great Lakes freighter or cargo ship.
5. Tell what the Soo Locks do, and why they are important.
6. Why were lighthouses built on the Great Lakes?
7. Which city is the largest port in Michigan?
8. Name two bulk cargoes that are often carried by ships on the Great Lakes.
9. Name several kinds of eating fish that come from the Great Lakes.
10. Why is fishing not as important today as it once was?

Words You Should Know

Here are words you should know before you read chapter 10.

Apollo	• ferry boat	Reuther, Walter
astronauts	• flu	Rickenbacker, Eddie
• communists	Germany	Roaring Twenties
• depression	Kennedy	Selfridge Field
• exhibits	• labor union	United Auto Workers
	• suspension bridge	Woodcock, Leonard

Chapter 10

THE TWENTIETH CENTURY

MOVING TO THE CITIES

Michigan has grown up over the years. At first, the Indian tribes were here alone. Then the pioneers moved in. Our great-great grandfathers and great-great grandmothers moved here. More people made Michigan their home.

In the 1830's and until the 1870's, most of the people lived and worked on farms. Others worked as lumberjacks. Many in the Upper Peninsula worked in mines and lived in mining towns. After 1900, more people moved to the cities and towns.

People moved to the cities for jobs. More and more factories were starting. They were making stoves, furniture, railroad cars, chemicals, cars and trucks. Michigan cities grew and grew. Michigan was becoming a state full of industry.

WORLD WAR I

In the years after 1900, our industries became even more important. There was trouble in Europe though. World War I had started. By 1917, the United States was helping to fight the war too! This was the biggest war the world had seen. Millions of people were fighting.

Men from Michigan went to Europe as soldiers. Women from Michigan went as nurses. Copper and iron were made into guns, bombs and ships.

Thousands of Michigan people had once lived in Germany. Now, Germany was the enemy. Sometimes the Michigan Germans were treated badly. But they were Americans now and they helped too.

Camp Custer was built near Battle Creek. Michigan soldiers went to train there. A terrible thing happened in 1918. Many of the soldiers became sick with the flu. It was a very dangerous kind of flu. Over 600 men died at the Camp.

Another camp was started at Selfridge Field. This was an airbase near Mt. Clemens. Eddie Rickenbacker trained there. He was a famous flyer in World War I.

Michigan factories sent much to Europe. Trucks were sent along with tanks. Car factories started to make airplane engines instead of cars. Even ships were built. They were sailed from the Rouge River. They were sent overseas too.

Men coming to join the army during World War I.

Henry Ford was against the war at first. He did not want to see so many people killed. He rented a ship and went to Europe. He tried to see the German leaders, but no one would talk to him. After a week, he could see it was useless. Many people thought he was foolish to try such a thing; but he said at least he had tried. It was a bold idea.

The people of Michigan tried hard to win the war. They went overseas to fight. Others stayed home to get the work done here. They worked in the mines. Men and women started working in the factories to help.

Finally, the war was over. The soldiers and nurses came home. Michigan factories began making millions of new cars. Better roads were built. This time was called the "Roaring Twenties." Everyone felt their troubles were over, and business was good.

But in 1929, a depression started. People stopped buying things. Factories closed down. Banks closed. Many people lost their savings in the banks. This was a very tough time.

AUTO WORKERS START A UNION

It was during these years that the auto workers started a union. A union is a group of workers who get together and talk with the owners of a factory about any problems. The workers often ask for better pay and working conditions. If they cannot make an agreement, the members of the union might go on strike. This means they will not work until the problems have been settled. There were not many unions then. The owners of the factories were against them. Some others did not think it was a good idea either. The workers wanted a say in how much they were paid. They wanted to have a say if people were fired. Today, most people feel unions are good. They keep the bosses from being too powerful. Unions help the workers have better jobs and more pay.

The United Auto Workers Union (U.A.W.) was started in 1935. Walter Reuther helped to start the union. He led it for many years. Later, Leonard Woodcock led the union. In 1936 there was a great strike. The workers decided not to work. They just stopped. It was called a sit-down strike. The workers stayed in the plant for days. This strike was in Flint. The governor and the United States President had to help stop the strike. After a while, the company and the union solved their problems.

Michigan now has some of the most powerful unions in the world. The auto workers have some of the highest pay in industry anywhere.

WORLD WAR II

In 1941, the Japanese attacked Pearl Harbor. After this, we were in World War II. Once more, Michigan men and women fought to keep freedom. They went to Europe and the Pacific. Many bombers were made here. The Willow Run Plant made the planes. They were flown all over the world to join the fight.

Thousands of brave Michigan people died fighting for freedom. Peace returned to Michigan and the world in 1945.

Tanks for the army were made in Michigan for World War II.

The years passed. Again our state grew. New buildings and highways were built. In 1957, the world's longest suspension bridge was built here. It kept this record for several years. This was the Mackinac Bridge. Many people call it the "Big Mac." The bridge is 8,614 feet long. It goes from the Lower Peninsula to the Upper Peninsula. Before the bridge was built, everyone had to use a boat to cross over. Ferry boats carried cars, trucks and people back and forth. Often there were long lines waiting to get across. The Mackinac Bridge helped bring the two parts of our state closer together.

Walter Reuther
(Michigan State Archives)

Leonard Woodcock
(Michigan State Archives)

103

WALTER REUTHER (ROO-ther)—A Union Leader (born 1907—died 1970)

Walter Reuther was born in West Virginia. His father came to America from a farm in Germany. Walter came to Detroit when he was nineteen. The year was 1927. He wanted to find a job in the automobile factories.

Soon he became a supporter of unions for auto workers. These millions of workers wanted better pay and shorter hours. He helped start the United Auto Workers Union (U.A.W.).

The early years of the union were not easy. There were fights with men hired by the companies. There were long strikes when the workers went hungry. They had no pay to use for buying food.

Bad people tried to take over the union. Criminals wanted the money, and Communists wanted the power. Walter Reuther fought hard to keep these people out. In 1948, someone fired a shotgun at him through his kitchen window. He lived, but he almost lost his arm.

Walter Reuther was elected president of the U.A.W. in 1946, and he was still president in 1970. That year he was killed in a plane crash. It was a loss to Michigan and the many people he had helped. Walter Reuther was another great man from Michigan.

LEONARD WOODCOCK—A Leader In Many Ways (born 1911—   )

Leonard Woodcock was born in Rhode Island. He arrived in Michigan in 1926. He went to Detroit City College.

In 1923 he started working at the Detroit Gear Company. While he worked there he joined the union. This is now called U.A.W. Local 42.

Mr. Woodcock became a union leader. In 1940 he was a representative for the U.A.W. He helped with U.A.W. groups around the world.

After Walter Reuther died, he was made the president of the U.A.W. He was president of the union for seven years before he retired. He was also on the Board of Directors for Wayne State University. Later, Leonard Woodcock became the United States Ambassador to China.

MICHIGANIANS GO INTO SPACE

The 1960's brought exciting ideas. President Kennedy started a plan to go to the moon. Many people were talking about outer space. Rocket ships were being built, and some parts for these were made in Michigan. The rockets did not take off from here. But some Michigan men went in them. Twelve of the astronauts have had some tie with Michigan.

Roger Chaffee (NASA)

James McDivitt (NASA)

Jack Lousma (NASA)

Al Worden (NASA)

Roger Chaffee was one of these men. He grew up in Grand Rapids. He was always interested in flying. While he was in college he studied engineering, and later joined the Navy. In 1963 he was one of a group of fourteen new astronauts. These astronauts had to do a lot of training. They had many tests to do. The astronauts were with the Apollo Program.

Roger and two others would be in the space capsule. In 1967, these men were testing the rocket and capsule. They were at the space center in Florida. The men were sealed in the capsule for a practice launch. It was like the "real" thing. Suddenly, Roger called out "Fire!" There was a bad fire in the spacecraft. In a few seconds the men were killed.

Roger Chaffee died being a pioneer. He faced danger in much the same way as the pioneers in early Michigan.

James McDivitt was an astronaut too. He is from Jackson, Michigan. He was on two space flights. He helped test the spacecraft that later went to the moon. Both of these men helped explore outer space.

Jack Lousma, who is from Grand Rapids, was the pilot of Skylab 2 in 1973. He and his crew spent many days in space doing special experiments.

Al Worden was born in Jackson. He was the command pilot for Apollo 15, which landed on the moon. Al and the other men with him explored the surface of the moon with the "moon rover."

In Jackson, Michigan, there is a space museum. It is called the Michigan Space Center. They have exhibits about space travel. There are also real rocket engines to look at and touch.

Chapter Review:

In this chapter you should have learned these important things:

   a. that after 1900, more people moved to the cities to find jobs, and this made the cities grow
   b. that in 1929 business became very bad which caused workers to lose their jobs and banks to close
   c. that this period of time was called the depression
   d. that Walter Reuther and Leonard Woodcock were the two men who helped start the United Auto Workers Union
   e. that bombers and tanks were made in Michigan during World War II
   f. what land is connected by the Mackinac Bridge and the year in which the bridge was finished
   g. that Michigan people have been a part of the space program

QUESTIONS TO ANSWER

1. Give some reasons why more and more Michiganians moved to the larger cities during the early part of the twentieth century.

2. What famous person from Michigan tried to stop World War I?

3. What things did the people of Michigan do to help win World War I?

4. What is the United Auto Workers?

5. Tell about Walter Reuther and Leonard Woodcock.

6. Name two things that were made in Michigan to help fight World War II.

7. In 1957 a bridge which was more than 8,000 feet long was built in Michigan. Name this bridge. What is connected by the bridge?

8. Give the names of two of the men from Michigan who helped start the space age.

Words You Should Know

Here are words you should know before you read chapter 11.

air conditioner	Dow, Herbert	perfume
Amway	Fremont	Post
aspirin	Gerber	• quarry (Kworee)
• brine	Kellogg	refrigerator
• bromine (BRO-meen)	• magnesium	saran wrap
Chelsea (CHEL-see)	Midland	Upjohn Company
doughnuts	Ontario (On-TAIR-ee-o)	vitamins

Chapter 11

INTERESTING PRODUCTS WE MAKE TODAY

You may be surprised about what is made in Michigan. Many things we see each day are made here.

Kellogg and Post cereals are made in Battle Creek. Corn flakes and many other kinds of cereal come from here. Battle Creek is the home of breakfast cereals. The first ones were made here.

Several kinds of medicine and vitamins are made in Kalamazoo. These are made by the Upjohn Company.

Saran Wrap and aspirin are made by the Dow Chemical Company. Their factory is in Midland. Some of their chemicals are made from salt water. This salt water comes from under the ground near Midland.

Salt is also mined under Detroit. There is a thick layer deep in the ground. This salt is used on roads. It melts the ice in the winter.

Pine trees are cut in our Upper Peninsula. They are used to make paper. Some Michigan wood is used to make newspapers. A little Michigan wood is used for furniture. These kinds are maple, walnut and oak.

Of course, cars are made here. Fords, Chryslers, Chevrolets and Oldsmobiles all come from Michigan. Army tanks are made in Detroit too. American Motors has its offices in Michigan. Several million cars are made here each year. Not all cars are made here, but many do come from Michigan.

Limestone comes from Michigan. The world's largest limestone quarry is in Rogers City. Limestone is used for building. It is used in fertilizer, and it is also used to make cement and glass.

Cement is made in Michigan. We even have a town called Cement City. Once there was a large cement plant there but now it is closed. Alpena produces it now.

Iron ore comes from the Upper Peninsula. It is made into iron and steel. Much of it goes into cars and trucks.

Michigan even has oil wells and gas wells. This fuel helps keep us warm in the cold winters. It is used to make the steel for the cars too. It gives the factories heat and electricity.

Many products are made at the Amway Company in Ada. They make soap, cleaning items, and even perfume.

Parts for refrigerators are made in Tecumseh. Air conditioners are made in

Jonesville and Addison. Flour for making doughnuts is made in Hillsdale. Gerber baby food is made in Fremont. Jiffy cake mixes and baking supplies are made in Chelsea.

Parts used in cars and trucks are made in many cities, not just Detroit. The car industry is statewide.

The Tony Tigers greet visitors at the Kellogg plant in Battle Creek. (Dave McConnell)

Herbert Dow (Michigan State Archives)

HERBERT DOW—Michigan's Chemical Pioneer (born 1866—died 1930)

Mr. Dow was born in Belleville, Ontario, Canada. His family had moved there from New England. Soon after he was born, they moved back to the United States.

Herbert Dow went to school in Ohio. In 1890 he came to Midland, Michigan. He wanted to test the brine there. Brine is salt water that comes from under the ground. The brine at Midland had other chemicals besides salt. One of these is bromine.

He started the Dow Chemical Company to take the bromine out of the brine and sell it. Soon he was able to take other chemicals from the brine too. These were used to make still other chemicals. Before long, the Dow Chemical Company produced over 400 products. Mr. Dow had more than one hundred patents in his name.

Today, the Dow Chemical Company makes Saran Wrap, aspirin, chemicals, cleaning products, magnesium metal and many more things.

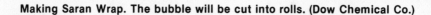

Making Saran Wrap. The bubble will be cut into rolls. (Dow Chemical Co.)

Chapter Review:

In this chapter you should have learned these important things:

   a. that Herbert Dow started the Dow Chemical Company, which makes many chemicals and is well known for making Saran Wrap and aspirin
   b. that Battle Creek is the city where breakfast cereal is made
   c. that the Upjohn Company in Kalamazoo makes different kinds of medicine
   d. that trees and iron ore are two important things from the Upper Peninsula
   e. that many people in Michigan earn a living from making cars and car parts
   f. what things are made in your city

QUESTIONS TO ANSWER

1. Will Kellogg and C. F. Post started a new product in Michigan. What was it, and where did they do this?

2. What company in Kalamazoo makes vitamins and medicines?

3. Where is the Dow Chemical Company?

4. Salt is mined under what Michigan city?

5. Trees from the Upper Peninsula are used to make what important product today?

6. What car companies are in Michigan today?

7. Where is the world's largest limestone quarry?

Words You Should Know

Here are words you should know before you read chapter 12.

Benton Harbor	dairy	strawberries
cucumbers	•festival	syrup—maple
•dahlia (DAL-ya)	sausage	• tart
		tulip

Chapter 12

GOOD THINGS TO EAT FROM MICHIGAN

When you are at the grocery store you can find all kinds of food from Michigan. Fruit, vegetables, meat and dairy foods are all from our state.

Cherries are grown here. They come from Traverse City and other towns near Lake Michigan. The water of the lake helps to make the weather just right for growing fruit. Michigan is the biggest producer of tart cherries in the United States.

Grapes are grown near Paw Paw. The grapes are used to make several things. They go into juice, jam and jelly. They are also used to make wine.

Apples and peaches are grown in several parts of Michigan. Some kinds of Michigan apples are famous for their good taste. In the summers many fine strawberries come from Michigan fields. The fruit market at Benton Harbor is probably the biggest in the world.

We grow beans around Saginaw and Bay City. So many beans are grown that we can not eat them all. We grow about eight times more than we use. What happens to the rest? They are sent to Europe on ships. More navy beans are grown here than in any other state.

Beets are grown in the thumb of the Lower Peninsula. These beets are not eaten in the way you may think they would be. They are sugar beets, and are used to make sugar. The sugar is just like the sugar from sugar cane, but it is from beets instead.

Michigan farmers grow more cucumbers than most states. The cucumbers are made into pickles. Much celery is grown near Kalamazoo.

The rich maple syrup you use on pancakes or waffles may come from Michigan. Michigan is one of the main maple syrup states. To make the syrup, sap is collected from maple trees. This is done in the early spring. The sap is almost like water, and it has to be boiled down to get rid of the extra water. After a long time, it thickens. When it is sweet enough, it is finished. The syrup is put into bottles and cans. You can visit places where the syrup is made. Fresh syrup is a taste treat!

Flower bulbs are grown in Holland, Michigan. Of course, these are not eaten. They are for flowers. Most of these are tulip bulbs. In the spring each year there are millions of tulips in bloom. They have many bright colors. Another kind of bulb is raised near Coloma. Here a Dutch family produces dahlia bulbs. They sell

Each year there is a national cherry festival in Traverse City. This boy is trying to win a contest by finishing his pie first. (Michigan Cherry Producers Association)

about five million dollars worth each year. That makes it a big business! These bulbs are sold in Michigan and other places.

We cannot forget Michigan cattle. They give us beef and milk. The dairy business brings Michigan farmers more money than any of the other animals that are sold, or any of the crops grown. It is the most valuable farm business here. Several years ago there was a real farm tragedy. A poisonous chemical was mixed with animal feed by mistake. This feed went to farmers all over Michigan. The chemical was PBB. It made the cattle sick. Some of the cattle even died. Later, people who ate the beef or drank the milk from these cows started to get sick also. Many people ate food with PBB. This happened because it was not discovered in time. Farmers had to kill their cattle so more people would not eat the poisoned food. This tragedy should teach us all to be very careful with chemicals. This is most important when the chemicals are used with things we eat.

Pigs and chickens are important on many farms. The pigs give us ham, bacon, pork and sausage. The chickens lay thousands of eggs.

Young people join the 4-H Club. Farm boys and girls who are in the 4-H often grow cattle and other animals to show at the county fairs. Many of them win blue ribbons for their work.

The farmers of Michigan give us good food to eat. They grow many kinds of food. Michigan has more kinds of food from its farms than many of the other states. We should be grateful to the farmers for the work they do for us.

Chapter Review:

In this chapter you should have learned these important things:
   a. that many of the things we eat are grown right here in Michigan
   b. that Michigan is famous for the growing of tart cherries and beans
   c. that we are well known for apples, peaches, strawberries and other fruit which is mostly grown near Lake Michigan
   d. that growing and selling flower bulbs is an important business
   e. that the most valuable farm business is dairy farming

QUESTIONS TO ANSWER

1. Michigan grows more of two foods than any other state. Name these.

2. Which of these are *not* important crops in our state: flower bulbs, apples, cotton, bananas?

3. What is the most valuable farm business in Michigan?

4. Michigan produces much sugar. The sugar is made from what plant?

5. What well-known product is made from tree sap?

6. Which Michigan city has one of the biggest fruit markets in the world?

Words You Should Know

Here are words you should know before you read chapter 13.

a justice (a judge)	graduated	Lindbergh, Charles
•congressman	historical markers	Los Angeles
divorced	Illinois	Motown sound
driver's license	lawyer	professional
Franklin, Aretha	license plates	Secretary of State
		university

Chapter 13

FAMOUS PEOPLE TODAY

How many famous people from Michigan can you think of? How often do you hear about people from our state in the news? Do you always know these people are from Michigan? There are probably more of these people than you think!

Gerald Ford was the 38th President of the United States. He and his wife, Betty Ford, grew up in Grand Rapids, Michigan. They are just two of the many famous people from our state. You will read more about them.

Michigan has also been the home of singers, actors, actresses, sports people, race car drivers and many more. There are so many people to talk about that we shall have to leave some out. Let us look at one group at a time. Here are the stories of several well-known people.

Gerald R. Ford, Jr., was the 38th President of the United States. Gerald Ford was born in Nebraska. His parents were divorced in 1915. His mother moved back to her parents' home in Grand Rapids.

President Gerald Ford and his wife on the back of a train. They were speaking to people to get votes.
(Ford Library—Ann Arbor)

Gerald was good at sports. He really liked football. He played center on the University of Michigan football team.

In 1935 he graduated from that university. After graduating, he decided to be a lawyer, but he needed more college for this. He went to Yale University for a law degree.

Meanwhile, World War II had started. In 1942, Gerald Ford joined the Navy. He served on an aircraft carrier. Once there was a great storm. Gerald was walking on deck and the ship tipped suddenly. He slid across the deck and almost fell into the sea. Five other men were washed away in that storm.

After the end of the war, he ran for Congress. In 1948 he was elected, and he served as a congressman from Michigan for many years. Gerald Ford was known for his hard work.

In 1973, the Vice President of the United States, Spiro Agnew, had to leave office. He had taken some money he should not have taken. President Nixon wanted Gerald Ford to become vice president. This he did. But President Nixon had also made serious mistakes. Soon he left office too. On August 9, 1974, Gerald Ford became President of the United States. He was the only president not to be elected by the people.

Gerald Ford ran for president in the next election, but he lost to Jimmy Carter. Mr. Ford served the people of Michigan and the nation well.

President Ford's wife, Betty, grew up in Michigan, too. Before she married, her name was Elizabeth Anne Bloomer. She was born in Chicago, Illinois. Her parents moved to Grand Rapids when she was two years old.

Betty Ford is well known for her common sense. She has often said what was on her mind. She talked to people about the problems she has had. This has helped other people to face their problems. She has spoken to many groups. Once a man died of a heart attack next to her at a meeting. She stayed calm and led a prayer for the man as he was carried away.

There is another man who is important to Michigan. You may have seen him on television asking people to drive safely or reminding them to renew their drivers' licenses. Do these clues help you think of his name? He is Richard Austin, the Secretary of State for Michigan.

The secretary of state is elected each four years. Mr. Austin has been doing a good job, and he has had this office for many years.

Richard Austin has other duties other than those dealing with drivers' licenses and license plates. He also is in charge of the History Division of the Department of State.

The people in this office manage the state museum in Lansing. They also place historical markers all over Michigan. You probably have at least one historical marker in your town. You should read any local markers you can find. See what is written on them and report to your class.

Mr. Austin is one of several Blacks who have worked their way to high political positions. Coleman Young, the mayor of Detroit, is another. These people deserve our thanks for the long hours they work and the hard problems they try to solve.

Who is Mary Coleman? She was the first woman in Michigan's Supreme Court. This is a very important and powerful position. She was made the Chief Justice because of her fine work. The Chief Justice leads the court. Before this, no woman had been the Chief Justice in Michigan.

The Supreme Court is the highest court in Michigan. Each year many interesting cases are tried in the Supreme Court. Often these cases affect all of our lives. The seven justices decide what the laws mean. They decide who is right and who is wrong.

Richard Austin

Mary Coleman

David Stockman

Charles Lindbergh (Michigan State Archives)

David Stockman is from Scottdale, Michigan. You may have heard about Mr. Stockman in the news. He helped President Ronald Reagan and worked in Washington, D.C. He was made the Director of the Office of Management and Budget (called OMB). His office works with the budget of the United States government. It helps decide how much money is spent and for what. David Stockman is another Michigan person who has been in the news.

Charles Lindbergh was born in Detroit. You should know why he is famous. He was the first man to fly across the Atlantic Ocean without stopping. He did this in 1927.

Many years ago, a man named Berry Gordy made records in Detroit. He found several good singers to help. They made the "Motown Sound." That was the nickname for it. Diana Ross, Stevie Wonder and Aretha Franklin were some of these singers. Diana Ross was one of the three girls in the singing group known as *The Supremes*.

The Supremes (Michigan State Archives)

Lily Tomlin and Marlo Thomas are two actresses from Michigan. They are two very funny ladies who often do comedy acts.

Mitzi Gaynor, actress, and George C. Scott, an actor, also lived here for a while. Mr. Scott was the tough actor who played the part of General Patton in a movie.

Ernest Hemingway lived near Petoskey in the summers. He was a famous writer. One of his books is about a river in the Upper Peninsula. It is called *Big Two Hearted River*. Many other writers are from Michigan. Some of these write about Michigan in their books. Edgar A. Guest was a famous poet. He often wrote a poem a day. His poems were printed in *The Detroit Free Press* for more than fifty years.

Gordon Johncock is a famous race car driver. He is also from Michigan. He is a winner of the Indianapolis 500 Race.

Many sports heroes are from Michigan. Others moved here to play on Michigan teams. Ty Cobb played for the Detroit Tigers long ago. He was one of the world's greatest baseball players. He was an expert hitter and base stealer. Al Kaline was on the 1968 World Series championship team. Mr. Kaline is a member of the Baseball Hall of Fame. Willie Horton was another famous Tiger baseball player. Denny McLain was a baseball pitcher. He won thirty-one games in one season!

Ty Cobb, the famous baseball player
from long ago.

Gordie Howe
(Hartford Whalers Hockey Club—Paul Kellogg)

Gordie Howe is one of the world's greatest hockey players. He was on the Detroit Red Wings team. Gordie Howe played hockey for more years than any other player. He holds many records.

Ervin "Magic" Johnson is from Lansing. He played basketball for Michigan State University. He helped the team win the N.C.A.A. title. After he left the university, he played with a pro basketball team.

All of these people help to make Michigan an interesting state in which to live. Many of them are world famous. When someone asks you where you are from, tell them Michigan. Be proud to be from Michigan. Tell them about all of the exciting people who have come from Michigan too!

121

Coleman Young talking with children. (City of Detroit)

Chapter Review:

In this chapter you should have learned these important things:

    a. that Gerald Ford was once President of the United States, and that he and his wife Betty are both from Grand Rapids

    b. that Mary Coleman was the first woman to be Chief Justice of the Michigan Supreme Court

    c. that David Stockman had an important job in Washington, D.C.

    d. who some of the well-known Michigan musicians, actors and actresses are

    e. who some of the famous sports people from Michigan are

QUESTIONS TO ANSWER

1. Who was the 38th President of the United States? In what Michigan city did he grow up?

2. List one interesting fact about the person in question one.

3. Elizabeth Anne Bloomer is better known by another name. What is this name?

4. Who was the first woman to be Chief Justice of the Michigan Supreme Court?

5. What city did the "Motown Sound" come from?

6. Name two famous singers from Michigan.

7. Name two actresses or actors from Michigan.

8. Tell what these people are known for: Charles Lindbergh, Gordie Howe, Willie Horton.

9. Tell which person from Michigan you would most want to be like. Please give your reasons.

Words You Should Know

Here are words you should know before reading chapter 14.

Ambassador Bridge	Grayling	Keweenaw Peninsula (KEE-wi-naw)
Belle Isle (Bell Eye ll)	Hackley, Charles	• lumber baron
Cobo Hall	Hartwick Pines	Renaissance Center (Ren-e-sans)
DeZwaan windmill	• interstate highway	• reservation
Dossin Museum	Ishpeming (ISH-pa-ming)	Tahquamenon Falls
Frankenmuth	Isle Royale (Eye ll ROY-el)	(Tah-KWAH-meh-non)
		• trolley

Chapter 14

PLACES TO TRAVEL—THINGS TO SEE

MICHIGAN'S HIGHWAYS

There are so many places to visit and things to do in Michigan. It is hard to believe they are all in our state. We have many good roads to use to get to them. Michigan has several interstate highways.

These highways are called interstates because they go from one state to another. They cross state lines. The interstate roads use numbers for their names. Three main interstate highways here are I-75, I-96 and I-94. They all have the "I" for interstate. See if you can find these highways on a map.

Highways built by the state have an "M" in the name, such as M-23. There are also roads with U.S. in the name. These were built by the United States government. US-2 and US-12 are roads of this type.

When you look on a map to find the roads, the numbers are in circles or shields. The circles are used for state roads, such as M-23. One kind of shield is used for U.S. roads. A different kind of shield is used for the interstate highways.

Now we will go on a trip around Michigan. We will see where many interesting places are to visit. This trip will start in Dearborn, which is near Detroit.

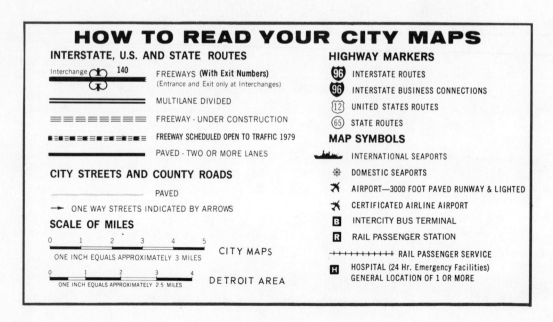

Part of the Michigan highway map. (Michigan Dept. of Transportation)

125

This old trolley still runs in Detroit. (Dave McConnell)

Dearborn is the home of the Ford Motor Company. Henry Ford's old home is here. Greenfield Village and Henry Ford Museum are in Dearborn too. These are near US-12.

Henry Ford started Greenfield Village and the museum. He wanted people to see what it was really like in the early days. He wanted people to see living history, not just history from books. The museum has many old things. It has real airplanes and steam engines inside. It has many early cars and machines.

Greenfield Village has houses and buildings from around the world. These buildings were taken apart and moved to Dearborn.

Thomas Edison's lab is here. The shop where the Wright brothers worked on their airplane is here too. There is a real steam train and a riverboat. Greenfield Village is a very exciting place to visit.

Now we will travel east on US-12 to reach downtown Detroit. Here there is the Renaissance Center. This is a new giant hotel and office building. Nearby is an old trolley. The trolley is like a bus on rails. You can ride the trolley past Cobo Hall and other famous places. Seventy-five years ago many people went to work on trolleys like this one.

If we turn around and follow the river the other way, we will pass the Ambassador Bridge and the Windsor Tunnel. Using the bridge and the tunnel, people go to Canada.

Not far away is Belle Isle. This is an island in the Detroit River. There is a park on Belle Isle. You can learn about sailing on the Great Lakes at Belle Isle, where the Dossin Great Lakes Museum is located. This museum has all kinds of things about ships.

For the next part of our trip, we will go north on I-75. We will drive past Flint. After a while, we will leave I-75 and go to Frankenmuth. Frankenmuth is a little German town. Every June there is a German festival in Frankenmuth. There are German shops here too. This town is well known for good places to eat. It also has a big company that sells Christmas decorations.

I-75 goes through Saginaw and Bay City. Soon we will reach Grayling. This is near the top of the Lower Peninsula. North of this town is Hartwick Pines. Hartwick Pines is a state park. People come here to see pine trees. These pine trees are special because they were not cut down by the lumbermen.

Hartwick Pines also has a museum. The museum shows the way the lumberjacks lived. It shows the saws, axes and other tools they used.

By going north on I-75 you reach the Mackinac Bridge. The bridge is hundreds of feet above the water. Ships sail far below under the bridge. Next to the end of the bridge is a fort. This is Fort Michilimackinac. It is the fort that was captured by Chief Pontiac's warriors.

St. Ignace is at the north end of the bridge. Mackinac Island is a small island nearby. Bois Blanc Island is a larger island east of the bridge.

Fort Mackinac is on Mackinac Island. It is a large fort on top of a hill. The fort was used for a long time, but today it is a museum too. Fort Mackinac has tall white walls. It has old cannons and they are still pointed out to the water. Once they were used to protect the fort.

Mackinac Island is an unusual place to visit. There are no bridges to the island. You must take a boat to get there. You can not take a car to the island. There are not even any cars on the island! They are not allowed. Everyone uses horses, wagons or bicycles!

I-75 goes across the Upper Peninsula. It is about fifty miles to Sault St. Marie, which is also called the Soo for short.

The Soo is next to Canada. On one side is Lake Superior. On the other side is Lake Huron. The Soo Locks are in between. These are the locks that thousands of ships use. The locks are needed because Lake Superior is higher. You can stand at the edge of the locks and watch the ships go by. They are only a few feet away!

Mighty Mac

Tahquamenon Falls

If we travel west on M-28, we will come to Marquette. It is 165 miles from the Soo. Before we come to Marquette, we will turn off this road. After about thirty miles, we will turn north on M-123. By going on this road, we can reach Tahquamenon Falls. (Sounds like tah-KWAH-meh-non.) Tahquamenon Falls is a very pretty place. There are really two waterfalls here. They are not as big as Niagara Falls; but they are still large. This is a good place to take pictures.

Starting on M-28 again, we come to Munising. Not far from Munising is Lake Superior. It is interesting to visit the lake shore near here. This shore is called the Pictured Rocks. It is rocky and high above the water. It is known as the Pictured Rocks because of the colors on the rocks.

Marquette is on Lake Superior too. There are iron mines near Marquette. These are at Negaunee and Ishpeming. The iron ore is brought to Marquette. In the harbor is a very big dock which is high in the air. Ships come next to the dock to be loaded. The ore is brought to the top of the dock by trains. The trains fill the bins in the dock. Next, the ore goes down a chute into the ships. You can watch this happening. Thousands of tons go into the ships. The ships go lower and lower in the water as the ore comes in.

Highway M-28 heads west. After a while it meets US-41. Highway US-41 goes north. Soon it goes through an Indian reservation. This is called the L'Anse Reservation. You will not see people with feathers in their hair living in wigwams. The tribes live in houses and have regular jobs. After going a short distance, we will be on the Keweenaw Peninsula.

This peninsula has two parts. There is water between them. We must cross a bridge to reach the end of the peninsula. At the tip is Copper Harbor. Early copper miners worked here. There is also a fort. This is Fort Wilkins. It was built in the early copper mining days, about 1844. It was supposed to protect the miners from the tribes but the Indians were friendly.

If you look northwest across the deep blue water, you might be able to see Isle Royale. It is about fifty miles into Lake Superior. Isle Royale is the part of Michigan that is farthest north.

Isle Royale is a rather wild place. There are many trees, moose and wolves there. It is a national park. In the summer, boats take people to visit the island. People hike and camp out. They look at the pretty wildflowers. They can hear the wolves call at night!

Let us pretend that we have a small airplane. Now we will take off and fly to the Sleeping Bear Sand Dunes. This is across Lake Michigan in the Lower Peninsula.

We will leave the Keweenaw Peninsula. We will cross Keweenaw Bay. Below us are the green forests of the Upper Peninsula. After a while, we will reach Escanaba. The plane will soon be over the water. Below is Green Bay.

As the Michigan shore gets closer, we can see two islands. These are North and South Manitou Islands. They are part of the Sleeping Bear Dunes National Lakeshore. Soon we can see the Sleeping Bear Sand Dunes. This is a very big hill of sand. There is only sand almost as far as the eye can see! It has this name because the tribes had a story about how the dune was formed. Their story is that a mother bear and her two baby cubs were swimming across Lake Michigan. The mother reached the shore safely and climbed to the top of the dune to wait for the cubs. The baby cubs, however, became too tired to swim all the way. They drowned in the lake. The mother bear still waits on top of the sand. She turned into the Sleeping Bear Dune while the cubs have become North and South Manitou Islands.

Now our pilot will go south along the shore. We fly over Point Betsie Lighthouse. We see smaller lakes. One of these is Crystal Lake, a beautiful place to vacation. The plane goes over Manistee and Ludington.

As we pass over Muskegon, we may see the home of Charles Hackley, a lumber baron. Years ago it was a very fancy house, but now it is a museum. Before long, we can look down and see a big windmill, the same kind that are in Holland. This

The windmill at Holland, Michigan. (Holland Chamber of Commerce)

windmill is in Holland, Michigan. It is several stories high. The windmill is called DeZwaan. This means the swan. The windmill is over two hundred years old. It was moved from the country of Holland in Europe, across the Atlantic Ocean.

It is time for the plane to turn east. We will fly close to Grand Rapids, our furniture capital. Downtown Grand Rapids has a big new hotel. It is very tall. There are other buildings too. A new museum in honor of Gerald Ford is in Grand Rapids.

131

Our plane will land in Lansing, the state capital. The big white dome of the capitol building can be seen for miles. Here the governor works. Our state laws are made in the capitol.

After the plane lands, you can visit the capitol building. There is a museum in the basement. You can walk by the door of the governor's office. Perhaps you can see him there!

You should find out if the members of the House or Senate are meeting. There is a place where you can go to watch them. It is on the second floor. The men and women are working below. Usually someone is talking. Probably they are talking about a law they would like to pass. The other members listen, and then talk too. When the talking is finished, a vote is taken. There is a board in front of the room that shows who votes. It shows if they vote for a bill or against it. A bill is the name for a law before it is voted on or passed.

This is a good place to end our trip around Michigan. You should now know how to read a road map. You should be able to find cities on the map and be able to see what roads to use to travel to them.

Remember some of the exciting places to visit in Michigan. There are many other places that we did not talk about. Maybe you can tell your class about places where you have been in Michigan.

Each year many people visit Michigan on their vacations. These people are tourists. They come to see our state. They often go swimming and camping or hunting. They also stay in motels and eat in restaurants. This brings business to the people who run the motels and restaurants. All of this makes the tourists and their business important to Michigan.

These pages tell a few of the interesting things in Michigan. You have learned about our history. You now know about the tribes and the first pioneers. You should remember some of the famous people who have made Michigan a great state, and some of the things these people did.

There are many things that do make Michigan a great state. One of these is YOU! Because you live here, Michigan is better for all of us. Be proud that Michigan is your home. Now you can tell others about the state where you live. Tell them about the exciting things you have learned!

QUESTIONS TO ANSWER

1. Tell about two things a person can see in or near Detroit.

2. What is the Renaissance Center and where is it located?

3. Which of these interstate highways go north and south, and which go east and west: I-75, I-96 and I-94?

4. Where is the Ambassador Bridge and Windsor Tunnel?

5. What does the Mackinac Bridge connect?

6. What was used by travelers before the bridge was built?

7. What road connects Sault Ste. Marie and St. Ignace?

8. Where are the Tahquamenon Falls?

9. Where are Isle Royale, Mackinac Island, Manitou Island and Belle Isle? (See the maps on pages 11 and 125 for help.)

10. Name the place in Michigan you would most like to visit. Tell why you want to go there. Look on a highway map and list the roads you need to use to drive there from your town.

A tourist family enjoying the beautiful state of Michigan.

GLOSSARY

The place to look for the meaning of a word or how to say it.

Admiral (AD-mer-al)—a high ranking officer in the Navy or Coast Guard.

Algonquian (Al-GON-kwee-in)—Indian language spoken by several tribes.

Archaeology (ARK-ee-oll-o-jee)—the study of how people lived long ago. It takes facts from things left behind by early people.

Assassinated (A-SAS-in-ate-ed)—the killing of an important person by a surprise attack.

Assembly line (a-SEM-blee)—a way of making cars and trucks as fast as possible. Each worker does the same job over and over. The car or truck moves by as it is put together.

Attorney General (eh-TER-nee)—the chief lawyer for the state.

Audubon Society (AW-DUE-bon)—A bird watcher's club; especially those who watch birds and animals and try to help the rare kinds.

Birch bark—bark from a birch tree which was sometimes used to make Indian canoes.

Bounty hunter—a person who hunts and tries to catch another person who is wanted. Then he is paid money if he can bring the wanted person back.

Brine—water that contains a great deal of salt, usually from under the ground.

Bromine (bro-meen)—a chemical that is usually seen as a deep red liquid giving off a strong smell.

Bulk—a kind of cargo shipped loose in a large container.

Canal—a man-made river for boats.

Capital (KAP-ih-tel)—the city where the main offices of a government are located. It is also the place where the laws are made.

Ceremonies (SER-eh-MO-nees)—special events that are always done the same way for an important reason. Example: When you finish high school you will be in a ceremony.

Cholera (KOL-er-a)—a dangerous sickness that can kill people.

Civil war—a war between two groups of people of the same country.

Coho Salmon—a small salmon. Some of this type of fish were brought from Oregon and Alaska and placed in the Great Lakes to improve the fishing.

Communists (KOM-you-nists)—people who support a type of government where the state owns all the businesses and almost everything else. The government runs practically everything. There is less freedom to do what a person wants to do.

Compass (KUM-pes)—a device with a magnetic needle that shows direction by pointing north.

Congressman—a member of the United States House of Representatives.

Coordinator (Ko-ORD-in-a-tor)—one who helps make something work together smoothly. A fashion coordinator helps people buy clothes that look nice together.

Counties—units of local government. A state is divided into many counties.

Courthouse—a building that holds the county government and its official records, such as deeds, birth and marriage records.

Customs (KUS-tems)—the habits as done for many years by the people of a country or area. It is a custom to have dinner about 6:00 p.m.

Dahlia (DAL-ya)—a tall plant that looks like a type of daisy, and is grown for its bright flowers.

Depression (dee-PRESH-on)—a time of very slow business when many people do not have jobs or money.

136

District (DIS-trikt)—part of a country, a state, or a city, marked off for a special purpose. Example: If you are in the first district, you will vote at the school.

Dolomite (DOLE-o-mite)—a hard white mineral that looks like limestone or marble.

Driver's license (LIE-sense)—a card given by the state showing that the person is old enough and has passed a certain test for driving a car.

Dynamite (DINE-a-mite)—a strong blasting powder used to blow up something.

Elk—a large animal like a deer with broad spreading horns that lives in the woods.

Executive Branch (eg-ZEK-eh-tiv)—one of the parts of government. The president and governor are in this branch.

Exhibit (ex-ZIB-it)—things put on display where people can go to see them.

Explorer (ex-SPLOR-er)—a person who travels over little-known lands, seas or outer space to find out about them.

Ferry boat—a boat that carries people, cars and goods across a river or lake when there is no bridge.

Festival (FES-tih-vul)—a party for a special event with many people, usually held each year. A Tulip Festival is held in Holland, Michigan.

Flu (floo)—a sickness much like a very bad cold.

Freighter (FRA-ter)—a ship used to carry goods or cargo, such as cars, coal, cement, etc.

Gem (jem)—a valuable stone which may be cut and polished for jewelry.

Gypsum (JIP-sum)—a mineral that is often white. It is used to make cement and plaster.

House, the—one part of the government made up of persons who have been elected to meet and make the laws for a state or country. The senate is the other part.

Infantry (IN-fen-tree)—the soldiers of an army who are trained to fight on foot. Example: The man is in the infantry not the airforce.

Interstate highway—a road that goes from a state to one or more other states. It is usually well paved for fast cars and trucks.

Jesuit (JEZ-oo-it)—a member of a religious group of men started in 1534.

Labor union—a group of workers who all want to have better working conditions and better pay for their jobs.

Land office—a government office where records are kept of the sale of government land. Pioneers went to the nearest land office to buy land and to record where it was located.

Locks—like a canal but with gates at each end used in raising or lowering boats as they pass from higher or lower lakes or oceans.

Log jam—when logs floating down the river to a sawmill pile into each other and become stuck in a way that the flow of the water will not carry them along.

Lumber baron (BEAR-on)—a rich or powerful lumbering person.

Magnesium (mag-NEE-see-em)—a light, silver-white metal. It can be made from brine.

Malaria (ma-LAIR-ee-eh)—a sickness caused by the bite of one kind of mosquito. It brings on a bad fever and chills that can cause death.

Massacre (MAS-ah-ker)—when many people are killed in a surprise attack.

Michigama (MISH-i-gama)—a Chippewa word meaning great lake. Michigan, the name of our state, comes from this word.

Mississippi River (Miss-eh-SIP-ee)—the longest river in the United States. It starts in Minnesota and flows mostly south and east until it reaches the Gulf of Mexico. Marquette and Jolliet first explored the upper part of the river.

Motto (MOT-toe)—a special group of words used to tell a main idea about a country, state, club, etc. The words are usually easy to remember. Example: *Be Prepared* is the Boy Scout motto.

Northwest Territory (TER-eh-TORY)—in the 1700's the land where Ohio, Indiana, Illinois, Michigan and Wisconsin are today was not yet made into states. The term, Northwest Territory, was used for all of this land. The states were formed later.

Nobel Peace Prize (No-BEL)—an award given each year to honor men and women who work to make life better for other people. Alfred Nobel was a rich inventor who left all his money for this prize.

Ordained (or-DANED)—the word used to show that a person has finished all the studies needed to become a preacher or priest and is ready to begin work with the church.

Partridge (PAR-trij)—a medium sized wild bird related to the chicken. It is hunted and used for food.

Pilothouse (PIE-let-house)—a small room on the deck of a ship where the steering wheel, compass, charts, etc., used to guide the ship are located.

Political party (poll-LIT-i-kel)—a group of people who take part in getting certain persons elected to run the government. The two main political parties in the United States are the Republican Party and the Democratic Party.

Ports—cities next to large rivers, lakes or oceans where ships load and unload.

Pouch—a small bag in which to carry things.

Quarry (KWOR-ree)—an open pit usually for mining stone, limestone or gravel.

Rapids—part of a river where the water flows very fast, sometimes over rocks often causing the water to foam.

Rawhide—made from the skin or hide of an animal, such as a deer. It is like leather.

Representative (rep-ri-ZENT-eh-tiv)—a person in the House section of the legislature who is elected to make laws. A representative serves only in the House, not in the Senate.

Republican Party (re-PUB-li-ken)—one of the two main political parties in the United States. It was first started to be against slavery. This party believes it is best to have less government control of people.

Reservation (REZ-er-va-shen)—the United States government set aside land where the Indians may live. This land is used only for this special purpose.

Revolution (rev-o-LU-shen)—when the people rise up and change their government by force.

Senate (SEN-et)—the part of the legislature with the fewer members. In the United States Senate each state has two senators.

Shanty boys (SHAN-tee)—men who worked cutting trees in the woods and lived in lumber camps. This is another name for lumberjacks. The term shanty boys was used first.

Shield (sheeld)—a piece of metal always in a certain shape used many years ago to protect the body during battles. There is a picture of a shield on our state flag.

Slavery (SLA-ver-ee)—the custom where certain people own other people. The slaves are usually made to do the hard work.

Stockade (Stok-AID)—a very tall and heavy fence made of wooden posts to keep out an enemy like in a fort.

Straits (strates)—narrow waterways connecting two lakes or oceans.

Sturgeon (ster-JUN)—a very large fish found in the Great Lakes.

Supreme Court (sue-PREEM)—the highest court. Each state has one and so does the United States. The state courts are for cases about state law.

Surveyor (sir-VA-er)—a person who measures a piece of land and makes a record of the measurements. Surveyors help people know where their land is located and where their neighbor's land starts.

Suspension bridge (SUS spen shen)—a type of bridge that hangs from heavy cables. The cables are held by tall towers that go into the sand under the water.

Symbols (SIM-bols)—special pictures that stand for something.

Tart—not sweet; sour.

Tipis (or tepee)—a tent shaped like a cone, covered with animal hides, and used as a home by some American Indians.

Ton—a measure of weight equal to 2000 pounds.

Townships—units of local government, many times containing 36 square miles. All of Michigan is divided into townships, except the large cities.

Trolley (TROL-ee)—a passenger bus that runs on tracks and gets its power from electrical wires above it.

Union (YOUn-yun)—the northern states in the Civil War. These states were against slavery, and they did not want the southern states to start their own country.

Warriors (WAR-eh-yours)—soldiers; sometimes Indian braves who protected the tribe.

INDEX